Answering Jehovah's Witnesses

Subject by Subject

Answering Jehovah's Witnesses

Subject by Subject

David A. Reed

 Baker Books

A Division of Baker Book House Co
Grand Rapids, Michigan 49516

© 1996 by David A. Reed

Published by Baker Books
a division of Baker Book House Company
P.O. Box 6287, Grand Rapids, MI 49516-6287

Seventh printing, March 2005

Printed in the United States of America

Library of Congress Cataloging-in-Publication Data

Reed, David A.
    Answering Jehovah's witnesses : subject by subject / David A. Reed.
        p.   cm.
    Includes bibliographical references and indexes.
    ISBN 0-8010-5317-X (pbk.)
    1. Jehovah's Witnesses—Controversial literature.   I. Title.
BX8526.5.R36   1996
289.9'2—dc20   96-1102

For current information of all new releases from Baker Book House, visit our web site:
http://www.bakerbooks.com/

Contents

Contents

Preface

If you are already familiar with my book *Jehovah's Witnesses Answered Verse by Verse* you might easily make a wrong assumption about *Answering Jehovah's Witnesses Subject by Subject*. You might assume that it is merely the same deck of cards reshuffled—the same material arranged according to subject rather than according to Bible verse. However, that is not the case. This book contains new and different material. It does not replace the verse by verse information. Rather, the two books complement each other and are meant to be used together.

Today's Jehovah's Witness door-knocker seems to be a bit less versed in Scripture than when my first book was produced and a bit more inclined to use arguments learned by rote at training sessions. So there is a real need for a book to help Christians deal with issues that do not lend themselves to verse-by-verse treatment. This book also responds to a number of surprising new arguments the sect has recently taught its members to use on unsuspecting Christians. Many of the chapters in *Answering Jehovah's Witnesses Subject by Subject* are adapted from articles in my quarterly *Comments from the Friends* that responded to these new Watchtower arguments as they were introduced over the past few years. In adapting these articles to book form I have also improved them with the help of feedback from readers who tested these approaches in the field.

Preface

During the decade since I wrote *Jehovah's Witnesses Answered Verse by Verse* it has been gratifying to see it translated into Spanish, French, Portuguese, and other languages and to see its combined printings approach a quarter-million copies. Yet, my greatest joy has come from seeing it used as an instrument in changing people's lives. Long ago I lost count of the letters that keep coming in. I've been able to put many of the JWs turning to Christ in touch with support groups, ministries, and sound Christian churches in their localities. And many have gone on to start outreach ministries of their own after getting on their feet spiritually and doctrinally.

How to Use This Book

How you may best use this book will depend on *why* you are using it and what you hope to accomplish. If your purpose is to enlighten yourself on Jehovah's Witnesses' beliefs and how to refute them, you can do this either by simply reading it from cover to cover as you would any other book or by turning first to the chapters that seem most interesting. If you are presently engaged in debate *versus* a JW adversary and need instant help on specific issues under discussion, find those subjects quickly using the alphabetically arranged headings or the Index at the back of the book. Each subject is developed independently of the others, so that there is no need to read the book from the beginning; cross-references in many of the sections will help you find related information that may prove helpful.

If your aim is to help a particular Jehovah's Witness realize that he or she is in the wrong religion, you would do well to take a different approach. Debating a JW on random subjects seldom accomplishes a complete overturning of that individual's religious thinking. Whether the argument is won or lost, the Witness remains a Witness. Your efforts could be compared to throwing your shoulder against a tree's limbs in the hope of toppling the tree. The exercise proves to be both painful and exhausting, but accomplishes nothing. To fell a tree you must cut through its trunk at the base. Then you hardly need to push it; it will fall under its own weight. Similarly with Watchtower thinking, if you cut through its foundation, the entire "tower" will fall.

So, instead of engaging in debate on a subject of the JW's own choosing or a subject that strikes your fancy, prepare first by reading the chapters on "Channel of Communication," "God's Organization," and "Mind Control." They will help you see how the Watchtower Society uses the weight of its supposed authority to uphold all sorts of unprovable doctrines, and how it uses techniques akin to brainwashing to manipulate the thinking of its followers. Then you will understand why the organizational doctrine—the teaching that the Watchtower Society is "God's organization" or "God's channel of communication"—needs to be cut down first. Moreover, you will see clearly the angle of approach that you must use so that your arguments will break through the brainwashing instead of being deflected by it.

The Watchtower leadership has instructed JWs *not* to listen to Christians who want to tell them about Jesus, *not* to debate doctrine with knowledgeable members of other churches, and *not* to read literature critical of the organization or its beliefs. On the other hand, they are trained to answer people's *questions* and to *help* people who need information. So, if you try to tell a Jehovah's Witness why his beliefs are wrong and yours are right, you will encounter fierce resistance, and the JW is likely to break off the discussion before you can make any progress. If, on the other hand, you *ask for help* and rephrase your arguments to present *the same evidence in the form of questions*, you will be able to accomplish a lot more. Working *with* the JW's brainwashing instead of struggling against it could be compared to the difference between swimming downstream and swimming upstream. You will be able to cover a lot more ground with a lot less effort.

What ground should you attempt to cover first? My experience is that most Christians want to start out proving the Trinity doctrine or the deity of Christ. However, my experience also is that those are the subjects least likely to produce results with JWs. The reason is two-fold: (1) The Watchtower has indoctrinated them more thoroughly on the matter of deity than on any other subject, and has trained them to pull dozens of Bible verses out of context to defend their position. (2) No matter how well you present your evidence for the Trinity or the deity of Christ, and no matter how convincing your arguments may be, the JW will reject whatever you say because it is coming *from you* instead of from "the channel of communication that God uses," namely "God's organization," the Watchtower Society. Even if your arguments are convincing, the JW sees them as very clever lies crafted by Satan, because he believes that you represent the devil's organization. The more convincing your arguments, the more likely the JW will view you as a dangerous opposer to be avoided in the future—just the opposite of what you would normally expect.

The solution to this problem is not to push harder on the Trinity and the deity of Christ, but rather to move the obstacle out of the way first. That obstacle is the Watchtower organization itself and the control that it exercises over the JW's mind. This "brainwashing" must first be dealt with *before* a Jehovah's Witness can reason logically on Scripture and other evidence in the same way that an ordinary person would reason.

Therefore, the best subjects to cover initially are those that undermine the JW's confidence in the Watchtower organization by revealing its prophetic failures, doctrinal flip-flops, and dishonest cover-ups. Only after he begins to see the sect's Brooklyn leadership as an unreliable guide can a JW begin to think for himself and reason logically on what Scripture actually says—rather than on what the Society *says* it says.

So, in a nutshell, the most effective method for leading a Jehovah's Witness to Christ requires that you avoid debating theological issues at first, and that you start out with well-planned questions rather than hostile arguments. Let the JW think he is teaching you while you ask questions that expose the Watchtower organization's failed prophecies, doctrinal flip-flops, and outright dishonesty. (Additional help in doing this may be found in my book *How to Rescue Your Loved One from the Watchtower.*) After you knock down the organization's perceived authority and turn off its mind control mechanisms, then you will be able more easily to lead the JW subject-by-subject through the doctrinal chapters of this book.

In any case, regardless of whether you are simply looking for ways to answer a Jehovah's Witness at your door or embarking on a serious mission to extricate a family member, *do not let the JW see this book.* A typical response to observing you with "apostate literature" such as this would be for a Witness to break off discussions and perhaps even to shun you henceforth as a dangerous "opposer." So, read it ahead of time or keep it where you can step out of sight to consult it, but avoid carrying in your hand a book JWs fear more than a loaded gun.

Subject by Subject
Answers for Jehovah's Witnesses

Abaddon

In his apocalyptic vision the apostle John saw an army of locusts ruled by "the angel of the bottomless pit, whose name in the Hebrew tongue is Abaddon, but in the Greek tongue hath his name Apollyon." (Revelation 9:11) Who is this angel of the bottomless pit? The Watchtower Society's 1917 commentary on Revelation titled *The Finished Mystery* explains the verse this way: **"Whose name in the Hebrew tongue is Abaddon.**—And he is 'a bad one,' sure enough.—2 Cor. 4:4. **But in the Greek tongue hath his name Apollyon.**—That is, Destroyer. But in plain English his name is Satan, the Devil." (page 159, emphasis in original) However, its 1969 commentary *Then Is Finished The Mystery of God* offers an entirely different explanation: "In the Hebrew his name is Abaddon, meaning 'Destruction'; and in Greek it is Apollyon, meaning 'Destroyer.' All this plainly identifies the 'angel' as picturing Jesus Christ, the Son of Jehovah God." (page 232)

What a dramatic reversal! It is difficult to imagine a more drastic change in teaching. The Watchtower organization identifies the angel of the bottomless pit first as Satan the Devil, and then as Jesus Christ. Jehovah's Witnesses today are familiar with the latter interpretation but generally unaware of the former.

Orthodox commentaries point out that the angel of the bottomless pit experienced a "fall" from heaven (Revelation 9:1) and hence classify him as demonic. But the goal in sharing this information with JWs would be not to persuade them of Abaddon's true identity, but rather to help them learn two more important lessons: (1) that their leaders employ the tyranny of authority in place of sound hermeneutics, simply asserting interpretations for followers to accept, and (2) that an organization guilty of confusing Satan with Christ can hardly be relied upon today for an answer to the vital question of who Jesus is.

See also Michael the Archangel.

Adam & Eve

Jehovah's Witnesses are trained to speak at great length about Adam and Eve when debating such matters as the nature of the soul and the principle of wifely subjection. But these are dead-end issues from the standpoint of sharing the gospel with them, hence inadvisable for Christians to pursue as topics for discussion. However, it may prove profitable to be aware of what the Watchtower Society has taught concerning the time interval between Adam's creation and Eve's. Though this may appear, at first glance, to be a piece of inconsequential trivia, it actually constitutes a significant piece of the puzzle that, when fully assembled, identifies the JW organization as a false prophet.

Adam and Eve figure prominently in the chronological calculations Watchtower leaders used during the late 1960s and early 1970s to promote their prediction that the world would end on or about October 4/5, 1975. Their theory was, in essence, that the six days of Genesis 1 are symbolic periods of seven thousand years each culminating in God's final creative act, the making of Eve from Adam's rib. The ensuing seventh day, God's rest day, must likewise be seven thousand years long. However, man's fall into sin in the Garden of Eden condemned humankind to six thousand years of toil, to be followed by a sabbath-like seventh thousand-year period of rest during the millennial reign of Christ. Adam was created on October 4th or 5th of the year 4026 B.C., so the story goes; thus, "According to this trustworthy Bible chronology six thousand years from man's creation will end in 1975, and the seventh period of a thousand years of human history will begin in the fall of 1975 C.E." (*Life Everlasting—in Freedom of the Sons of God*, Watchtower Society, 1966, page 29)

Released at conventions of Jehovah's Witnesses in the summer of 1966, the book featuring this prophecy created quite a stir among them, especially since it went on to say, "It would not be by mere chance or accident but would be according to the loving purpose of Jehovah God for the reign of Jesus Christ, the 'Lord of the Sabbath,' to run parallel with the seventh millennium of man's existence." (page 30) This implied, of course, that the world would end and God's kingdom would come in the autumn of 1975.

The time interval between Adam's creation and Eve's came into play because the Bible is silent on how long Adam remained alone before God made his helpmate. The August 15, 1968 *Watchtower* article titled "Why Are You Looking Forward to 1975?" draws a direct connection between this time interval and the world's end:

Are we to assume from this study that the battle of Armageddon will be all over by the autumn of 1975, and the long-looked-for thousand-year reign of Christ will

17

begin by then? Possibly, but we wait to see how closely the seventh thousand-year period of man's existence coincides with the sabbathlike thousand-year reign of Christ. If these two periods run parallel with each other as to the calendar year, it will not be by mere chance or accident but will be according to Jehovah's loving and timely purposes. Our chronology, however, which is reasonably accurate (but admittedly not infallible), at the best only points to the autumn of 1975 as the end of 6,000 years of man's existence on earth. It does not necessarily mean that 1975 marks the end of the first 6,000 years of Jehovah's seventh creative "day." Why not? Because after his creation Adam lived some time during the "sixth day," which unknown amount of time would need to be subtracted from Adam's 930 years, to determine when the sixth seven-thousand-year period or "day" ended, and how long Adam lived into the "seventh day." And yet the end of that sixth creative "day" could end within the same Gregorian calendar year of Adam's creation. It may involve only a difference of weeks or months, not years. [page 499]

The article goes on to explain that ". . . Eve was created after Adam. So not until after this event did the sixth creative day come to an end." But it adds that ". . . the lapse of time between Adam's creation and the end of the sixth creative day, though unknown, was a comparatively short period of time." (page 500)

So, Jehovah's Witnesses expected that if the battle of Armageddon failed to occur in the autumn of 1975 it would still happen a "short" time later, in a matter of "weeks or months, not years." Elsewhere, in fact, the Watchtower Society assumes Eve was created in the same year as Adam. Thus its 1971 Bible dictionary *Aid to Bible Understanding* comments, "At the age of 130 another son was born to her. Eve called his name Seth . . ." (page 538) This, of course, is the same age Genesis 5:3 assigns to Adam at the time of Seth's birth. And the 1974 book *God's "Eternal*

Purpose" Now Triumphing for Man's Good places the year 526 B.C. "3,500 years from creation of Adam and Eve" (pages 131–132) and specifically states that the "seventh creative 'day' begins, 4026 B.C.E." (page 51) Alert JWs saw all of this as further confirmation that the battle of Armageddon should end this old world and bring in Christ's millennial reign by the autumn of 1975.

When that failed to happen and the years 1976 and 1977 found us—I joined the sect in 1969—still trudging from house to house offering the same literature to the people at the doors, we would answer householders' questions about 1975 with the explanation that the interval between the creation of Adam and Eve must have been a bit longer than we had assumed, and that this pushed back the start of Christ's thousand-year reign by a corresponding period of time. Nearly seven years after the 1975 failure, when my wife and I left the organization in 1982, that explanation was becoming a bit far-fetched. And now, in the mid–1990s, it would require that Adam lived a full twenty years alone, before the creation of his mate—quite a bit longer than the "weeks or months, not years" allowed by the 1968 *Watchtower* article titled "Why Are You Looking Forward to 1975?" At this point it would be appropriate to ask Jehovah's Witnesses instead, "Why are you still following the Watchtower?"

Adventist Origins

Frequently encountering critics as they ring bells and knock on doors up and down residential streets across the land, Jehovah's Witnesses are accustomed to defending themselves against the charge that they are "upstarts, just a new religion started by some religious crank recently and without a good background."[1] Their official response has often been to the effect that "Jehovah's witnesses are the most ancient religious group of worshipers of the true God, the people whose history runs back farther than any religious denomination of Christendom, or even of Jewry."[2] In fact, their book *Jehovah's Witnesses in the Divine Purpose* amplifies upon this by asserting that "Jehovah's witnesses have a history almost 6,000 years long, beginning while the first man, Adam, was still alive," that Adam's son Abel was "the first of an unbroken line of Witnesses," and that "Jesus' disciples were all Jehovah's witnesses too." (pages 8–9)

An outsider listening to such claims quickly realizes, of course, that the sect has simply appropriated unto itself all the characters named in the Bible as faithful witnesses of God. By such extrapolation the denomination is able to stretch its history back to the beginnings of the human family—at least in the eyes of adherents who are willing to accept such arguments. But outside observers generally dismiss this sort of rhetoric and instead reckon the publication of the first issue of *Zion's Watch Tower* in July, 1879, as the birth of the Jehovah's Witness sect.

It was born at that time, not as an only child, but as part of a large family of Adventist denominations spawned by the Millerite movement of the early 1800s. William Miller was a Baptist lay preacher who, in 1816, began proclaiming that Christ would return in 1843. His predictions captured the imagination of thousands in Baptist and other mainline churches. Perhaps as many as 50,000 followers put their trust in Miller's chronology and prepared to welcome the Lord while, as the appointed time approached, others watched nervously from a distance. Recalculations moved the promised second advent from March, 1843 to March, 1844, and then to October of that year. Alas, that date too passed uneventfully. After the "Disappointment of 1844" Miller's following fell apart, with most of those who had looked to him returning to their respective churches before his death in 1849. Other disappointed followers kept the movement alive, although in fragmented form, and their activities eventually led to the formation of several sects under the broad heading of "Adventism." These included the Advent Christian Church, the Life and Advent Union, the Seventh-Day Adventists, and various Second Adventist groups—one of which later split to form the Watch Tower movement.

The end of the Civil War in 1865 found former Millerites promoting new dates for the Second Coming. George Storrs of Brooklyn, New York, who published the *Bible Examiner* and was instrumental in forming the Life and Advent Union, focused his followers' hopes on 1870, while a group headed by N. H. Barbour of Rochester, New York, looked to 1873 or 1874, and published their calculations in Barbour's periodical the *Herald of the Morning*. Storrs was also a "conditionalist," teaching that men do not have immortal souls, but that everlasting life is attained on the condition of receiving this gift from God. Barbour and Storrs were among the Adventist leaders who shaped the thinking of a newcomer to the religious scene, teenager Charles Taze Russell.

Born on February 16, 1852, in Pittsburgh, Pennsylvania, Russell was 11 years old when the battle of Gettysburg raged, a day's horseback ride from his home, leaving some 45,000 men dead or wounded. Originally raised a Presbyterian, he was 16 years old and a member of the Congregational church in the year 1868 when he found himself losing faith. He had begun to doubt not only church creeds and doctrines, but also God and the Bible itself. At this critical juncture a chance encounter restored his faith and placed him under the influence of Second Adventist preacher Jonas Wendell. Russell later wrote:

Seemingly by accident, one evening I dropped into a dusty, dingy hall in Allegheny, Pa., where I had heard religious services were held, to see if the handful who met there had anything more sensible to offer than the creeds of the great

21

churches. There, for the first time, I heard something of the views of Second Adventists, the preacher being Mr. Jonas Wendell . . .

—*Zion's Watch Tower,* July 15, 1906,
page 3821 Society's reprints

For some years after that Russell continued to study Scripture with and under the influence of various Adventist laymen and clergy, notably Advent Christian Church minister George Stetson and the *Bible Examiner's* publisher George Storrs. He acknowledged this later in life:

Thus I confess indebtedness to Adventists . . . And here I should and do gratefully mention assistance rendered by Brothers Geo. Stetson and Geo. Storrs, the latter the editor of *The Bible Examiner,* both now deceased. The study of the Word of God with these dear brethren led, step by step, into greener pastures . . .

—*Zion's Watch Tower,* July 15, 1906,
page 3821 Society's reprints

As time went on he began meeting locally on a regular basis with a small circle of friends to discuss the Bible, and this informal study group came to regard him as their leader or pastor.

In January 1876, when he was 23 years old, Russell received a copy of the *Herald of the Morning,* N. H. Barbour's magazine. One of the distinguishing features of Barbour's group at that time was their belief that Christ returned invisibly in 1874, and this concept presented in the *Herald* captured Russell's attention. It meant that this Adventist splinter group had not remained defeated, as others had, when Christ failed to appear in 1874 as predicted; somehow they had managed to hold onto the date by affirming that the Lord had indeed returned at the appointed time, only invisibly. Was this mere wishful thinking, coupled with a stubborn refusal to admit the error of failed chronological calculations? Perhaps, but Barbour had some arguments to offer in support of his assertions. In particular, he came up with a basis for reinterpreting the Second Coming as an invisible event:

> It seems that one of Barbour's group had come into possession of Benjamin Wilson's *Diaglott* translation of the "New Testament." He noticed, at Matthew 24:27, 37, 39, that the word rendered *coming* in the King James Version is translated *presence* in the *Diaglott*. This was the clue that had led Barbour's group to advocate, in addition to their time calculations, an invisible presence of Christ.
> —*Jehovah's Witnesses in the Divine Purpose*, page 18

The Greek/English interlinear translation titled *The Emphatic Diaglott* had first been published by its author, Benjamin Wilson, a newspaper editor of Geneva, Illinois, in 1864. Regarding his religious affiliations the Jehovah's Witness *Awake!* magazine's predecessor *Consolation* says

> Mr. Wilson was reportedly a Christadelphian. Christadelphians believe the organized churches are apostate, do not believe in the "trinity", do not believe in the "inherent immortality of the soul" or in "eternal torment", but hold that eternal death is the punishment awaiting the wicked. Though free from these basic errors, they are in bondage to religion . . .
> —November 8, 1944, page 26

However, other sources[3] acknowledge that Benjamin Wilson was a personal friend of John Thomas, who founded the Christadelphians, but they identify Wilson as a member of the "Church of God (Faith of Abraham)."

In any case, the group headed by N. H. Barbour seized on Wilson's translation to escape the disappointment other Second Adventists experienced in 1874. Instead of coming up with an new date, they came up with a new interpretation of Christ's return as an invisible "presence." The idea appealed to young Charles Taze Russell, but others apparently refused to accept the story of an invisible Second Coming, with the result that the *Herald of the Morning* was failing financially.

In the summer of 1876, Russell paid N. H. Barbour's way to Philadelphia and met with him to discuss both beliefs and finances. The upshot was that Russell became the magazine's financial backer and was added to the masthead as an Assistant Editor, contributing articles for publication as well as monetary gifts. His small study group similarly became affiliated with Barbour's.

They all, including Russell, believed that Christ's invisible return in 1874 was to be followed by other predicted events, most notably that "the living saints would be suddenly and miraculously caught away bodily" to be with the Lord three-and-a-half years later in the spring of 1878. (*Zion's Watch Tower,* July 15, 1906, page 3823 Society's reprints) When this expected Rapture failed to occur on time, the *Herald*'s editor, Mr. Barbour, came up with "new light" on this and other doctrines. Russell, however, rejected some of the new ideas and persuaded other members to oppose them. Finally, Russell, as he himself explained,

> withdrew entirely from the *Herald of the Morning* and from further fellowship with Mr. B. . . . that I should start another journal in which the standard of the cross should be lifted high . . .
>
> —*Zion's Watch Tower,* July 15, 1906,
> page 3823 Society's reprints

He titled his new magazine *Zion's Watch Tower and Herald of Christ's Presence* and published its first issue with the date July, 1879. In the beginning it had the same mailing list as the *Herald of the Morning* and considerable space was devoted to refuting the latter on points of disagreement.

At this point Charles Russell no longer wanted to consider himself either an Adventist or a Millerite. But he still saw Miller and other Adventist leaders as instruments of God in fulfilling prophecy. In the *Watch Tower*'s third year of publication he wrote

> For the sake of many new readers of the WATCH TOWER, it may not be amiss to give a general review of the steps of faith by which the Lord has been leading us as a people, during the last seven years, and in a general sense during the preceding thirty-five years.
> —*Zion's Watch Tower*, November, 1881, page 288 Society's reprints

Seven years before 1881 would be 1874, and 35 years before that would be 1839. So, when he spoke of "us as a people" during the years since 1839, Russell could not have been limiting his remarks to the Watch Tower movement he founded in 1879; rather, in saying "us" he must have included the Millerites and Adventists. Some months earlier he had written of "the advance of the knowledge of truth for ten years past," adding that "Looking back to 1871, we see that many of our company were what are known as Second Adventists." (*Zion's Watch Tower*, February, 1881, page 188 Society's reprints) Also, he wrote concerning Jesus' parable of the ten virgins

> While we are neither "Millerites" nor "Adventists," yet we believe that this much of this parable met its fulfillment in 1843 and 1844, when William Miller and others, Bible in hand, walked out by faith on its statements, expecting Jesus at that time. . . . A brother, Barbour of Rochester, was we believe, the chosen vessel of God through whom the "Midnight Cry" issued to the sleeping virgins of Christ, announcing a discrepancy of thirty years in some of

25

Miller's calculations . . . and the Bridegroom due in that morning in 1874. . . .

If these movements were of God, and if Bros. Miller and Barbour were his instruments, then that "Midnight Cry," based on the prophetic and other statements and evidences, was correct, and the "Bridegroom came" in 1874. We believe that Midnight Cry was of God . . .
—*Zion's Watch Tower,* November 1881,
pages 288–289 Society's reprints

Thus Russell continued to view Miller and Barbour as instruments chosen by God to lead His people. Although Jehovah's Witnesses today think of Russell as the *first* in a succession of leaders, earlier Watchtower publications present Russell as the successor of N. H. Barbour:

Pastor Russell took the place of Mr. Barbour who became unfaithful and upon whom was fulfilled the prophecies of Matt. 24:48–51 and Zech. 11:15–17.
—*Studies in the Scriptures,* Vol. VII, *The Finished Mystery,* 1917 edition, page 54

Strangely, though, Jehovah's Witnesses today do not see themselves as an Adventist sect of Christendom, with their founder Charles Taze Russell a successor to previous Adventist leaders. Thus a recent article in their *Awake!* magazine (October 22, 1989, pages 17–21) refers to the Seventh-Day Adventists as "the largest of some 200 Adventist denominations" and adds that "The Adventists stem from Baptist lay minister William Miller's movement of the early 1840's." Later the article goes on to discuss the beginnings of Jehovah's Witnesses, but without any hint that the JWs also stem from the Millerites and are therefore closely related to the Seventh-Day Adventists. Discussions in other recent Watchtower publications indicate that the Witnesses are the only "true followers of Christ" totally separate from "Christendom's religions." (*Mankind's Search for God*, 1990, page 346)

The discussion of Russell's religious affiliations in the Society's 1993 history of the JW movement, *Jehovah's Witnesses—Proclaimers of God's Kingdom* contains some of the information related above but fragments it into separate discussions on pages 43–48, 120–122, 132–135, and 204. So, when the book concludes on page 204 that

> The operation of the organization of Jehovah's Witnesses has undergone significant changes since Charles Taze Russell and his associates first began to study the Bible together in 1870

readers may have forgotten that Russell actually remained a part of the Adventist organization until 1879, as revealed in the earlier material, and that therefore a separate "organization of Jehovah's Witnesses" was not operating at all in 1870 when Russell was still an Adventist teenager.

See Christendom *and* Russell.

AIDS

Outsiders may be surprised to find that Jehovah's Witnesses have so much to say in their publications about AIDS (Acquired Immune Deficiency Syndrome). For example, their *Watchtower Publications Index 1986–1990* devotes nearly a full page of small print listings to the subject, with some two hundred individual references to the sect's books and magazines. Why so much about this disease? One of the last entries under "AIDS" on page 16 of that *Index* reveals the reason: "best prevention is to become one of Jehovah's Witnesses," it says, referring readers to specific quotes to that effect. The different references, it turns out, actually feature the identical quote repeated in different *Awake!* magazine articles: "Professor Vincente

Amato Neto, Brazilian expert on infectious diseases, says: 'I often say that the best prevention for AIDS is for one to become one of Jehovah's Witnesses, for the members of that religion are neither homosexuals nor bisexuals, they are loyal to their marriage—they associate it with reproduction—don't use drugs and, to complete the picture, they don't accept blood transfusions.'" (October 8, 1988, page 15; also, May 8, 1988, page 29)

Much the same could be said, of course, for *any* denomination or sect adhering to biblical moral standards—with the exception of the last point, the JW abstinence from blood transfusions. But is joining the Witnesses actually the "best prevention" for AIDS?

As might be expected of such a claim, the Watchtower Society makes this assertion without offering any supporting statistics. Perhaps the quoted Brazilian professor accepts at face value the image of JWs promoted by the sect's public relations personnel. But my own observation during thirteen years as an active Witness leads me to a different conclusion. During my eight years as one of the overseers of our hundred-odd member congregation, the body of elders I sat on had to deal with more cases of fornication and adultery than I can remember, plus a smaller number of homosexual cases, a handful of members involved in substance abuse, and even one case involving a young man selling drugs at one of our Kingdom Hall meetings. Was this Massachusetts congregation uniquely troubled? Apparently not, in view of *The Watchtower*'s admission, in a different context, that "even some who have been prominent in Jehovah's organization have succumbed to immoral practices, including homosexuality, wife swapping, and child molesting" with "36,638 individuals" expelled in 1985 as unrepentant wrongdoers, "the greater number of them for practicing immorality," and "over 40,000" expelled in 1991 (January 1, 1986, page 13;

November 15, 1991, page 9) These JWs, as well as additional thousands who engaged in such conduct but repented so as to avoid expulsion, would all have been at risk of acquiring the AIDS-causing HIV virus just as much so as non-JWs involved in the same sort of conduct.

But, what about the matter of refusing blood transfusions? When the medical community began having a problem with HIV-positive blood donors and AIDS-contaminated blood, Jehovah's Witnesses began pointing to this as evidence that they had been right all along in refusing blood transfusions.

"AIDS-contaminated blood is a toxic substance," *Awake!* magazine declared in a brief article titled, "'Toxic' Blood," about a doctor who contracted the virus from an improperly discarded syringe. (March 8, 1989, page 29) Yet, it was not really the blood that was toxic, but rather the virus contaminating it. Not only blood, but *all* body fluids and tissues of AIDS carriers become dangerous to the extent that the HIV virus is present. Does the existence of contaminated water prove that people should avoid drinking clean water? Does the existence of contaminated food prove that people should avoid eating clean food? If not, then the existence of contaminated blood can not be used as an argument against transfusions—especially with improved methods for screening contaminated donors.

The most startling aspect of the situation, however, is the fact that Jehovah's Witnesses themselves can get AIDS and do indeed get AIDS from contaminated blood products they *do* take. Although rejecting "transfusions of whole blood, red cells, white cells, platelets, or blood plasma," (1990 booklet "How can blood save your life?" page 14) the Watchtower Society permits its followers to receive such blood products as Factor VIII (for hemophiliacs), Rh immune globulin (for pregnant women with Rh incompatibility), albumin (for shock), and various blood serums (antitoxins) to fight disease. The Society acknowledges that Witnesses taking such blood products face "health risks involved in an injection made from others' blood." (*The Watchtower*, June 1, 1990, pages 30–31)

So, contrary to the impression given in some of their publications, Jehovah's Witnesses run the risk of getting AIDS just like the rest of the population, and the "best prevention" is to avoid possible sources of infection rather than to "become one of Jehovah's Witnesses."

Alcyone

Alcyone is the name of the brightest star in the Pleiades cluster. For many decades *Watchtower* readers believed that God inhabited this star—that Alcyone was God's home. J. F. Rutherford's book *Reconciliation* speaks of the Pleiades with the thought "that one of the stars of that group is the dwelling-place of Jehovah." (page 14) Which star in particular? Many of Rutherford's readers would have called to mind an earlier publication of the Watchtower Society, Russell's *Studies in the Scriptures*, Volume 3, which refers to "Alcyone, the central one of the renowned Pleiadic stars . . . from which the Almighty governs his universe." (page 327)

In 1953 the Society reversed this teaching, declaring instead that "it would be unwise for us to try to fix God's throne as being at a particular spot in the universe." (*The Watchtower*, November 15, 1953, page 703) Then, in 1981, the Society made another reversal, returning to the original view that God has a place of residence: "God being an individual, a Person with a spirit body, has a place where he resides, and so he could not be at any other place at the same time." (*The Watchtower*, February 15, 1981, page 6) Only now the sect's leadership has held back from naming Alcyone as that place.

See Pleiades.

Apostates

Apostates, as Jehovah's Witnesses use the term, are former members who now reject the Watchtower Society's teachings. Outsiders might assume, from the revulsion and disdain JWs manifest at the mere mention of these former members, that such apostates have rejected God, Christ, the Bible, and everything Christian morality stands for. But this generally is not the case. Rather, the ex-members assigned the apostate label are usually those whose zeal for God and whose depth of biblical scholarship has led them to question some of the sect's unorthodox teachings.

In the "Questions from Readers" column (page 31) of its April 1, 1986 issue *The Watchtower* makes an unusual admission of this fact. The column responds to a reader's inquiry, "Why have Jehovah's Witnesses disfellowshipped (excommunicated) for apostasy some who still profess belief in God, the Bible, and Jesus Christ?" The official answer includes the following:

> Approved association with Jehovah's Witnesses requires accepting the entire range of the true teachings of the Bible, including those Scriptural beliefs that are unique to Jehovah's Witnesses. What do such beliefs include? . . .
>
> That there is a "faithful and discreet slave" upon earth today "entrusted with all of Jesus' earthly interests," which slave is associated with the Governing Body of Jehovah's Witnesses. (Matthew 24:45–47) That 1914 marked the end of the Gentile Times and the establishment of the Kingdom of God in the heavens, as well as the time for Christ's foretold presence. . . . That only 144,000 Christians will receive the heavenly reward. . . .

Thus individuals who are exemplary in moral conduct and in their activity as Jehovah's Witnesses may be expelled as apostates for questioning the 1914 date or the number of those going to heaven or, more significantly, the authority of the JW Governing Body to make such determinations.

For obvious reasons, the article fails to mention that, between 1967 and 1980, Witnesses could also face disfellowshipping for violating the "unique" belief that organ transplants were forbidden by God as a form of cannibalism. (*See* Organ Transplants.) And, that between 1972 and 1978, married couples could be disfellowshipped for violating the Governing Body's "unique" beliefs about what sort of contact was improper between husband and wife in the marriage bed. (*See* Marriage.) When the organization itself later abandoned these "unique" beliefs, it made no apology to the individuals who had earlier been disfellowshipped. They retained the apostate label for having questioned the organization's authority.

JWs often bring up the subject of apostates when a non-Witness they are talking with challenges them on the sect's failed prophecies, doctrinal flip-flops, or other embarrassing facts about the organization. "Where did you get this information?" they typically ask. "Have you been talking to apostate ex-Witnesses or reading books by apostates?" Since Witnesses find exposés of their organization's blunders much more unsettling and more threatening to their faith than biblical arguments, the Brooklyn leadership has taught them to dismiss all such information out of hand with the argument that it must have come from apostate ex-Witnesses.

Apostates are the most despicable people on the face of the earth, JWs are taught, with the result that a Witness would much rather encounter someone expelled from the sect for theft or adultery than find himself face-to-face with an apostate. *The Watchtower* tells them that they "must hate" apostates and that they must not be "curious about apostate ideas." (October 1, 1993, page 19) Therefore, any information that may come from an apostate source can be dismissed without even listening to it.

This method of dealing with a charge by attacking its source is what debaters call an *ad hominem* argument—one directed at the man rather than at his ideas. In another context not dealing with apostates, the JW *Awake!* magazine itself lists "Attacking the Person" among the "Five Common Fallacies" in argumentation and concludes, "But while personal attacks, subtle and not so subtle, may intimidate and persuade, never do they disprove what has been said." (May 22, 1990, pages 12–13)

If a Jehovah's Witness attempts to use the "apostate source" argument to dismiss questions you raise about the organization, what is the most effective response? Scripture says, "He that answereth a matter before he heareth it, it is folly and shame unto him." (Proverbs 18:13) But the JW would say this proverb does not apply to apostates any more than it would require us to give the devil a full hearing every time he showed up. We already know the devil is a liar, and apostates are in the same class as Satan himself. The JW usually needs to see first that the Watchtower Society is not "God's organization" before he or she can even begin to think about apostates without a blinding emotional reaction.

Rather than try, at this point, to change the JW's view of apostates and their ideas, appeal instead for the Witness to help *you* settle the questions in *your* mind. Explain that *you* need to determine who is right, the JWs or the ex-JWs, and that the only way *you* can do this is by examining the evidence offered by both sides. Explain that, if the Witness refuses to listen or refuses to respond to what the apostates are saying, this would leave you with the impression that the apostates may be right. Explain that you would have to conclude that the Witnesses are resorting to *ad hominem* arguments due to lack of a better response.

In most cases, however, it is best to avoid the problem in the first place. When you raise issues about the organization to make JWs start questioning their faith, base your discussion on information you obtain from neutral third-party sources at the public library or information you are able to draw out of the Witnesses themselves. Never let the JWs see that you are consulting this book or others by former Witnesses.

See Censorship *and* Mind Control.

Appointed Times of the Nations

A fixed time period of 2520 years, stretching from October 607 B.C. to October 1914 A.D., is referred to in the Bible as the "times of the Gentiles" or "appointed times of the nations" (Luke 21:24 KJV, NW) according to Watchtower teaching. Witnesses believe the Gentile Times were set by God to foretell exactly when Jesus Christ would be installed as king in God's kingdom. The last Jewish king in the royal line of David was dethroned in 607 B.C., so the story goes, and the next king in that line would be the Messiah Jesus who could not begin to rule until the Gentile nations had held uninterrupted sway over the earth for seven prophetic "times" of 360 years each, or a total of 2520 years. (7x360=2520) Thus Jesus would be enthroned in October 1914.

Since JWs believe that this enthronement took place in heaven and was invisible to people on earth, it might seem to be a moot point or an irrelevant subject of mere academic interest. Not so, however, because they also believe[*] that event to have triggered a final generation-long countdown to the end of the world—"the Creator's promise of a peaceful and secure new world before the generation that saw the events of 1914 passes away." (*Awake!*, February 22, 1994, page 4) Quick mental arithmetic reveals that the events of 1914 occurred more than 80 years ago as of this

---

[*]As this book was going to press, the Watchtower Society instructed JWs to drop this belief. (*See* False Prophets, *footnote.*)

writing, and most members of a generation pass away before they reach 80 years of age, so the world's end must be imminent. Moreover, since Jehovah's Witnesses are the only religious group sounding this specific warning, they must logically be the ones God has picked to survive the end of the world. Thus it behooves would-be survivors to join the Watchtower organization.

This line of argument, used daily by JWs at the doors of prospective converts around the world, highlights the importance of what the sect teaches about the "appointed times of the nations." Their pitch for converts stands or falls on that doctrine. So, is it valid?

That question actually requires examination of a number of component teachings which, like links of a chain, join together to form the doctrine of the "appointed times of the nations." As with a literal chain, the doctrine will prove to be no stronger than its weakest link. Since the Watchtower Society uses the date 607 B.C. as the starting point, that first link needs to be examined closely.

The organization teaches that Jerusalem was desolated in 607 B.C. by Babylonian armies under King Nebuchadnezzar. However, the conquest of the Jews by the neo-Babylonian empire is a major event of Middle Eastern history of interest not only to Jehovah's Witnesses but also to secular historians, and these experts assign the year 587 B.C. to the events the Watchtower says happened in 607. Why the difference? It is a *very* long story. JWs who accept the Watchtower Society's word as authoritative but who want to examine the evidence to the contrary may wish to read the 226 pages of explanation in *The Gentile Times Reconsidered* by Carl Olof Jonsson (La Jolla, Calif.: Good News Defenders, 1983), but most other observers will see as highly questionable the Witnesses' use of a starting date at odds with the history books. The "chain" starts out with a very weak link indeed.

What about what might be termed the "middle" link, namely the 2520 year time span the Watchtower Society assigns to the "appointed times of the nations"? Jesus gave no such time period at Luke 21:24. Rather, the Society derives it by combining together several widely scattered Bible passages: (1) King Nebuchadnezzar's dream that the prophet Daniel interpreted to signify "seven times" of madness for the king (Daniel 4:16–32) is used to supply the number seven. (2) The 1260 days of Revelation 11:3 are presented as being equal to the "time, and times, and half a time" of Revelation 12:14, which are said to add up to three-and-a-half "times." Now if 3 1/2 times=1260 days, then 7 times=2520 days. (3) The 2520 days are converted to 2520 years by using the formula "each day for a year" at Ezekiel 4:6. Thus the JWs arrive at a time period of 2520 years. However, the problem is that the passages employed to achieve this end are totally unrelated. There is no sound basis for pulling the number seven out of an event in Nebuchadnezzar's life, the 3 1/2 times and 1260 days out of an unrelated prophetic symbol in Revelation, and the "day for a year" formula out of Ezekiel, and then combining them with Jesus' words at Luke 21:24. This combination of verses taken out of context produces a result that suits the Watchtower's purposes, but the process is no more valid than combining Matthew 27:5 with Luke 10:37 to produce the admonition, "he . . . went and hanged himself," so, "Go, and do thou likewise." The alleged 2520-year time period is another weak link in the chain.

The final link of chain in the JW "appointed times of the nations" doctrine is the concluding date of October 1914. Watchtower founder Charles Taze Russell learned the date as a young man from Adventist preachers whose services he attended and whose writings he studied. Then he himself went on to write that "the seven times will end in A.D. 1914" in his 1876 article titled, "Gentile Times: When Do They End?" in the Adventist magazine *Bible Examiner*—

three years before he began publishing his own *Watch Tower* magazine. Thus JWs point to this 1914 date as a rock-solid foundation of their chronology that they have been teaching for well over a hundred years.

But the facts are that they have totally changed their view of the *significance* of 1914. They formerly taught that "the time of the end" began in 1799 and would conclude in 1914; today they believe it began in 1914. They used to teach that Christ returned invisibly in 1874 and would take control of earth's affairs in 1914; now they believe he returned in 1914. They long predicted "the full establishment of the Kingdom of God in the earth at A.D. 1914" (*Studies in the Scriptures*, early editions of Vol. 3, page 126); now they say the kingdom was set up *in heaven* at that time and will assume earthly power later. Virtually everything they formerly taught concerning 1914 has been changed, making it another weak link in the chain.

The context of Jesus' words at Luke 21:24 reveals that he was speaking concerning the destruction of Jerusalem by the Gentile Romans and prophesying concerning the Jews—"this people" (verse 23)—that "they shall fall by the edge of the sword, and shall be led away captive into all nations: and Jerusalem shall be trodden down of the Gentiles, until the times of the Gentiles be fulfilled." There is no indication whatsoever that he was referring back to the Babylonian destruction, nor that he was pointing to a fixed time period ending in 1914. JWs accept the Gentile Times teaching on the strength of the Watchtower Society's supposed authority to speak for God, but outsiders find no support in Scripture for such an interpretation.

See Chronology.

Armageddon

It is only to be expected that a sect preoccupied with endtimes prophecies would focus much of its attention on the battle of Armageddon. Scripture associates the term with "the battle of that great day of God Almighty" when God will war against "the kings of the earth and of the whole world" at "a place called in the Hebrew tongue Armageddon." (Revelation 16:14, 16 KJV) Jehovah's Witnesses have always spoken out boldly to sound the warning about this time of judgment, but they have not spoken in agreement over the years.

Watchtower founder Charles Taze Russell was very clear on the subject. He taught, "The date of the close of that 'battle' is definitely marked in Scripture as October, 1914. It is already in progress, its beginning dating from October, 1874." (*Watch Tower*, January 15, 1892, page 1355 reprints) He saw Armageddon as a battle lasting forty years, ending with the world's end in October 1914. (*See* Appointed Times of the Nations.)

As the forty years were about to end, however, he changed his mind and revised his teaching to say that the battle was yet future: "Armageddon may begin next spring, yet it is purely speculation to attempt to say just when." (*Watch Tower*, September 1, 1914, page 5527 reprints) Then, as the First World War ignited and spread, he began to identify it as the fulfillment of Revelation's prophecy: "The present great war in Europe is the beginning of the Armageddon of the Scriptures." (*Pastor Russell's Sermons*, 1917, page 676)

Russell died before World War I ended, but his successor Joseph F. Rutherford used the occasion of the Second World War to speak of "the remaining months before Armageddon." (*The Watchtower*, September 15, 1941, page 288) Those months had already stretched into decades when *The Watchtower* featured an article titled "Why Are You Looking Forward to 1975?" in which it asked, "Are we to assume from this study that the battle of Armageddon will be all over by the autumn of 1975, and the long-looked-for thousand-year reign of Christ will begin by then?" It answered, "Possibly," then briefly reviewed some of the supposed evidence and concluded, "It may involve only a difference of weeks or months, not years." (August 15, 1968, pages 494, 499)

Alas, those months too have again stretched into years and even into decades. True Christians are no less eager than Jehovah's Witnesses for the apocalyptic endtimes prophecies to be fulfilled. The difference is that Christians study the *whole* Bible rather than focus narrowly on certain verses highlighted in Watchtower publications. Thus we recall that the Lord also said, "But of that day and hour knoweth no [man], no, not the angels of heaven, but my Father only." (Matthew 24:36 KJV) Jesus also said, "You also must be ready, because the Son of Man will come at an hour when you do not expect him." (Luke 12:40 NIV) The Lord encouraged us, not to try to calculate ahead of time just when he would return, but rather to be ready as if he might come at any time. We eagerly await the world's end and the coming of God's kingdom, but without attempting to set a date.

See False Prophecies *and* False Prophets.

Baptism

Jehovah's Witnesses broke their own prior record established in New York City in 1958 when their August 1993 convention in the former Soviet Ukrainian city of Kiev saw 7,402 new members baptized. (*The Watchtower,* January 1, 1994, page 9) Reports in the secular media presented these baptisms as differing only in quantity from those performed in Baptist churches or at the worship services of others who similarly practice immersion. That there is a more significant difference becomes apparent, however, when it is noted that the Witnesses *rebaptize* converts who were immersed earlier in another church. A closer look at their procedure helps explain why.

For many years the Watchtower organization baptized candidates after they publicly answered *yes* to these two questions: (1) "Have you repented of your sins and turned around, recognizing yourself before Jehovah God as a condemned sinner who needs salvation, and have you acknowledged to him that this salvation proceeds from him, the Father, through his Son Jesus Christ?" and, (2) "On the basis of this faith in God and in his provision for salvation, have you dedicated yourself unreservedly to God to do his will henceforth as he reveals it to you through Jesus Christ and through the Bible under the enlightening power of the holy spirit?" (*The Watchtower*, May 1, 1973, page 280) This was the formula followed when I was baptized at a JW circuit assembly in Plymouth, Massachusetts, in the spring of 1969.

But in its issue of June 1, 1985, *The Watchtower* magazine presented new questions to replace those used previously. These new questions are as follows: "On the basis of the sacrifice of Jesus Christ, have you repented of your sins and dedicated yourself to Jehovah to do his will? Do you understand that your dedication and baptism identify you as one of Jehovah's Witnesses in association with God's spirit-directed organization?" (page 30)

Comparison with the old questions reveals that this new formula eliminates the thought of salvation through faith. It also replaces the idea that God might reveal His will "through Jesus Christ and through the Bible" by means of the Holy Spirit, with a new focus on "God's spirit-directed organization."

The old formula bore at least some resemblance to the biblical injunction to baptize disciples "in the name of the Father and of the Son and of the Holy Spirit." (Matthew 28:19 NIV, NKJB, RSV) The revised wording, however, removes JW baptism even farther from the biblical pattern, transforming it into an organizational membership commitment rather than a relationship with God. This may be acceptable to persons indoctrinated to believe that "identifying themselves with Jehovah's organization is essential to their salvation." (*Our Kingdom Ministry*, November 1990, page 1) But such a baptism is offensive to those who see Christ as the true Savior and as the only one to be obeyed as Lord. Any organization inserting itself into the picture as essential to salvation and demanding obedience must be viewed as a false savior and lord, a corporate false Christ, and thus one of the "false Christs, and false prophets" that Jesus warned against. (Matthew 24:24)

Beth-Sarim

Hebrew for "House of the Princes," this is the name of a Watchtower mansion built in San Diego, California, in 1929 and eventually sold in 1948. The purpose of its construction has been a matter of some controversy, with various JW publications offering different explanations.

The house was built "for Brother Rutherford's use," according to the *1975 Yearbook of Jehovah's Witnesses*, when his doctor advised the Society's second president to spend his winters in a warmer climate away from New York.

In contrast to this, the 1942 book *The New World* indicates it was built to house pre-Christian men of faith who the Witnesses expected would be raised from the dead at that time: ". . . those faithful men of old may be expected back from the dead any day now. . . . In this expectation the house at San Diego, California . . . was built, in 1930, and named 'Beth-Sarim,' meaning 'House of the Princes.' It is now held in trust for the occupancy of those princes on their return." (page 104) The 1930 deed to the property actually names King David, Gideon, Barak, Samson, and others as the intended residents of Beth-Sarim, with the Society holding it in trust for them. (See photostatic copy of the deed on pages 54–56 of the book *Eyes of Understanding* by Duane Magnani, Witness, Inc.)

Which was the true purpose for Beth-Sarim? Was it built as a winter home for the Society's president? Or as a dormitory for soon-to-be-resurrected princes? Rutherford was the one who actually occupied the house, along with a staff of servants. He died there in January of 1942. But imagine how well the news would have been received during the Great Depression that this nonprofit New York religious organization was maintaining a California mansion for the benefit of its chief executive! Hence the story was put out during the 1930s and early '40s that the building was constructed for the "princes." As the years passed, however, the Society's prediction that those men would be resurrected "any day now" proved to be a false prophecy. Holding Beth-Sarim "in trust for" them became a graphic reminder of that false prophecy. To remove this source of embarrassment, the property was sold in 1948. When reference was made to it afterward, it was now more acceptable to say simply that it had been built "for Brother Rutherford's use."

The Watchtower Society's latest history book, *Jehovah's Witnesses—Proclaimers of God's Kingdom* published in 1993, features a photo of the mansion on page 76 and says more about it than any other JW publication of the past fifty years. It indicates Beth-Sarim was built to give J. F. Rutherford a warm climate to winter in due to a bad lung. Next it quotes from the Society's 1939 book *Salvation* to the effect that "the purpose of acquiring that property and building the house was that there might be some tangible proof that there are those on earth today ... who believe that the faithful men of old will soon be resurrected by the Lord, be back on earth, and take charge of the visible affairs of earth." Then it goes on to say in a footnote that "At the time, it was believed that faithful men of old times, such as Abraham, Joseph, and David, would be resurrected before the end of this system of things and would serve as 'princes in all the earth,' in fulfillment of Psalm 45:16. This view was adjusted in 1950 . . ." But the book leaves the uninitiated reader wondering just what the connection was between the mansion and the princes. It fails to state that the house was intended for their occupancy and that the deed named the Old Testament judges rather than "Judge" Rutherford.

This subject is one worth bringing up in conversations with Jehovah's Witnesses, since the Watchtower Society still falls short of telling the whole truth about Beth-Sarim.

Bible

"Yes, I believe that the Bible is inspired by God, that it is inerrant, and that it is the final authority for believers." A Jehovah's Witness will readily express agreement with this view of Scripture. Besides that, the Watchtower headquarters complex in Brooklyn, New York, has publicly displayed for decades a large sign encouraging daily Bible reading. Why, then, are JW doctrines at such variance with what other Bible readers believe? The difference is due to another aspect of their view of the Bible that they do not immediately discuss with outsiders, namely, their belief that "the Bible is an organizational book. . . . For this reason the Bible cannot be properly understood without Jehovah's visible organization in mind." (*The Watchtower*, October 1, 1967, page 587)

JW leaders have pointed the finger at the Roman Catholic Church, charging that the "religious hierarchy of the Vatican . . . belittles Bible study by the common people . . . by claiming that it is the only organization authorized and qualified to interpret the Bible." (*The Watchtower*, July 1, 1943, page 201) Yet the Watchtower Society makes the identical claim for itself by saying that God "wants his earthly servants united, and so he has made understanding the Bible today dependent upon associating with his organization." (*The Watchtower*, November 1, 1961, page 668) "He does not impart his holy spirit [*sic*] and an understanding and appreciation of his Word apart from his visible organization." (*The Watchtower,* July 1, 1965, page 391) ". . . the fact is that we cannot understand the Bible on our own. We need help. . . . Jehovah, through his organization, however, has allowed his loyal servants to understand its meaning today." (*The Watchtower,* October 1, 1994, page 6)

In fact, my own personal departure from the sect, which was after I had begun doing independent Bible reading, was triggered by this statement that I saw as an attempt to elevate the organization above the Bible: ". . . Jehovah God has also provided his visible organization . . . Unless we are in touch with this channel of communication that God is using, we will not progress along the road to life, no matter how much Bible reading we do." (*The Watchtower,* December 1, 1981, page 27) I was so offended by this putting down of the Bible that I wrote the first issue of my newsletter *Comments from the Friends* in response. The organization, in turn, put me on trial for publishing independently and ordered that I be expelled and shunned.

Although I had not yet made contact with ex-Witnesses and was unaware of other dissent within the organization, I learned later that independent Bible study groups at Watchtower headquarters were broken up during the early 1980s as part of an Inquisition-type purge that eventually culminated in the expulsion of Governing Body member Raymond Franz. (*Time* magazine, February 22, 1982, page 66)

Ironically, the organization has attacked such former members with the charge that independent Bible reading led them to adopt the very doctrines that orthodox Christian churches teach and that Jehovah's Witnesses reject:

> . . . from among the ranks of Jehovah's people . . . haughty ones . . . say that it is sufficient to read the Bible exclusively, either alone or in small groups at home. But, strangely, through such "Bible reading," they have reverted right

back to the apostate doctrines that commentaries by Christendom's clergy were teaching 100 years ago.

The Watchtower, August 15, 1981,
pages 28–29

Loyal followers, on the other hand, see themselves as the only people on earth who truly study the Bible in a worthwhile manner. They view their referring to scattered verses quoted and cited in Watchtower publications as superior to reading the Bible by itself, because the true doctrines cannot be discerned from the Bible alone: "Let us face the fact that no matter how much Bible reading we have done, we would never have learned the truth on our own. We would not have discovered the truth regarding Jehovah, his purposes and attributes, the meaning and importance of his name, the Kingdom . . ." (*The Watchtower,* December 1, 1990, page 19)

Strange indeed! The Watchtower Society, in the last two statements quoted, has admitted that people who read the Bible alone end up believing the teachings of the orthodox churches rather than the unique doctrines of Jehovah's Witnesses.

The fallacy of the Witnesses' approach is revealed by the constant need to replace Watchtower literature with "corrected" material containing "new light." (*See* New Light.) The literature JWs view as "the truth" today becomes obsolete tomorrow. Books twenty-five or thirty years old are no longer used, and those from the late 1800s and early 1900s are viewed as containing so much error that they have often been removed from Kingdom Hall libraries and new members are cautioned against reading them. The biblical interpretation found in those older publications bears little resemblance to what Jehovah's Witnesses believe today. (See my book *Jehovah's Witness Literature—A Critical Guide to Watchtower Publications,* Baker Book House, 1993.) Christians who read the Bible itself, on the other hand, find the same precious truths their parents, grandparents, and great-grandparents found there, because "the word of the Lord endureth for ever." (1 Peter 1:25)

See also New World Translation, *for information about alterations in the official JW version of the Bible.*

Birthdays

Children in kindergarten and the early grades look forward with delight to celebrating birthdays—their own and their classmates'—throughout the school year. But these class parties are dreaded occasions for JW children who must leave the room or sit out the celebration without participating. They are taught that "Jehovah's Witnesses do not share in birthday festivities" because such "tend to give excessive importance to an individual . . ." (*School and Jehovah's Witnesses*, page 18) Adult Witnesses who have violated this ban have been summoned for trial before a church court and expelled for the simple act of sending a birthday card.

The organization's rationale for taking such a strong stand is based largely on Genesis 40:20–22, "the third day, which was Pharaoh's birthday . . . he made a feast unto all his servants . . . But he hanged the chief baker," and Matthew 14:6–10, "when Herod's birthday was kept, the daughter of Herodias danced before them, and pleased Herod. . . . And he sent, and beheaded John in the prison." Their thought is that the word *birthday* appears in the Bible only in reference to these pagan rulers, Pharaoh of Egypt and Herod of Galilee, both of whom put someone to death in connection with the celebration. Since men of faith are not recorded in the Bible as having celebrated their birthdays, but only such evil men—so the Watchtower reasoning goes—Jehovah's Witnesses today should not celebrate birthdays either. Rather than leave it for the individual Witness to read the Bible and reach this conclusion, the sect's

Governing Body has promulgated its official interpretation as *God's law* and uses its disciplinary procedures to enforce the policy.

Surprisingly, however, *The Watchtower* magazine celebrated its own 100th birthday. The July 1, 1979, *Watchtower* was a "special issue" titled "Keeping Watch For 100 Years," commemorating the magazine's birth in July of 1879. And when the Pennsylvania corporation publishing the magazine became 100 years old in 1984, it too had a celebration: "A special occasion indeed! . . . it was appropriate that Jehovah's Witnesses should mark this centennial of the Watch Tower Society by a special gathering." (*The Watchtower*, January 1, 1985, page 16)

Do the sect's leaders who partied on their own centennial have sound biblical reasons for denying children such parties on their birthdays?

It should be noted that Pharaoh and King Herod, cited by JWs as reasons for the ban, were arbitrary rulers and violent men. They were accustomed to executing people whenever it suited them, not just on their birthdays. Moreover, a person sending a birthday card, or a parent providing a cake with candles at a children's party, can hardly be accused of following the pattern of those murderous men.

Although the actual word birthday appears only in connection with Pharaoh and Herod in most translations, the Bible does contain reference to such celebrations in godly families. At Job 1:4, the JW *New World Translation* says of the patriarch Job, "And his sons went and held a banquet at the house of each one on his own day; and they sent and invited their three sisters to eat and drink with them." That *his own day* refers to each one's birthday becomes clear when we read further, "It was after this that Job opened his mouth and began to call down evil upon his day. Job now answered and said: 'Let the day perish on which I came to be born.'" (Job 3:1–3) Thus, the *Living Bible* renders Job 1:4–5 this way: "Every year when each of Job's sons had a birthday, he invited his brothers and sisters to his home for a celebration. On these occasions they would eat and drink with great merriment. When these birthday parties ended—and sometimes they lasted several days— Job would summon his children . . ."

Furthermore, the Watchtower Society's own *New World Translation* reveals that the birth of John the Baptist was an occasion to be celebrated, when it records this angelic announcement: "And you will have joy and great gladness, and many will rejoice over his birth." (Luke 1:14)

In years gone by, when *Watchtower* readers were more diligent at reading the Bible itself than JWs today, they had a custom of using the Society's *Daily Heavenly Manna* book to keep "a list of birthdays." (*Jehovah's Witnesses—Proclaimers of God's Kingdom*, page 201) The Society's founder and first president Charles Taze Russell saw nothing wrong with the practice. All of the evidence weighed together indicates that the sect's more recent leaders who have banned birthday celebrations have done so on their own authority rather than for any compelling biblical reason.

See Christmas *and* Holidays.

Blood Transfusions

The most frightening aspect of the Jehovah's Witness religion, from the viewpoint of the man on the street, is members' refusal to accept blood transfusions even in the face of certain death. Newspaper headlines such as, "Jehovah's Witness Refuses Blood, Dies," appear with grim regularity in cities around the globe. Even more public attention is captured when JW parents battle in court to block a child's desperately needed medical treatment, or when they remove a sick youngster from the hospital and flee to avoid a court-ordered transfusion.

Why do Witnesses place their lives and their children's lives in jeopardy? Because the Watchtower Society tells them God requires it. Obviously, there is no specific mention of transfusions in the Bible, since the medical technique was not developed until more than a thousand years after the New Testament was completed. Blood itself is mentioned, however, and JW publications interpret biblical references to blood as implying a divine ban on transfusions. Most notably they see in the admonition to "abstain . . . from blood" at Acts 15:20 and 29 a permanent apostolic injunction against the medical use of blood or blood products.

References to blood in the Bible actually center around two areas: diet and sacrifice. In the Old Testament, Noah and his offspring were commanded not to eat the blood of animals they killed for food. (Genesis 9:4) The nation of Israel was repeatedly instructed not to eat blood, because this portion of their animal sacrifices was set aside for God: "Moreover ye shall eat no manner of blood, whether it be of fowl or of beast, in any of your dwellings. Whatsoever soul it be that eateth any manner of blood, even that soul shall be cut off from his people," (Leviticus 7:26–27) because "the blood of thy sacrifices shall be poured out upon the altar of the LORD thy God, and thou shalt eat the flesh." (Deuteronomy 12:27) The prohibition against "eating" blood would include intravenous feeding, Watchtower leaders reason; hence transfusions come under the ban.

In quoting such Old Testament verses, however, they ignore another prohibition commonly found right alongside the prohibition on eating blood, namely, God's command to the Jews not to eat any fat either: "Ye shall eat no manner of fat, of ox, or of sheep, or of goat." (Leviticus 7:23) The prohibition against eating fat was intended to be just as permanent as the dietary ban on blood. "It shall be a perpetual statute for your generations throughout all your dwellings, that ye eat neither fat nor blood." (Leviticus 3:17) Yet Jehovah's Witnesses who carefully avoid foods containing blood have no objection whatsoever to

49

eating fat. Is this, perhaps, a clue indicating that the Watchtower Society is feeding them verses out of context?

Later, in the New Testament, the apostles sent a letter out to all the Christian churches instructing them to "abstain" from blood. (Acts 15:20, 29) This abstinence would preclude taking blood in any manner, the Watchtower Society explains, even through the veins; and instructions from the apostles to all the churches must remain in force for Christians today. However, if that were so, then how could Paul a short time later tell Corinthian Christians they were free to eat whatever meat their pagan neighbors or markets were offering? (1 Corinthians 8:1–13) Again, the Society has ignored context. The apostles sent out their letter to settle a dispute that had arisen in the churches. Most Christian churches at that time consisted of a nucleus of Messianic Jews, plus a growing number of Gentile converts. The Gentiles put faith in the Jewish Messiah, but disputes developed over whether or not they also had to get circumcised and keep the Law of Moses with its kosher diet. The inspired apostolic letter was aimed at addressing this contemporary issue rather than banning an as yet unknown medical procedure two thousand years in the future.

Do the various Old and New Testament verses about blood actually require that believers refuse transfusions in life-threatening situations? Jehovah's Witnesses are virtually alone in interpreting Scripture this way. Orthodox Jews who insist upon kosher meat—slaughtered and bled under rabbinic supervision—have no objection to blood transfusions. Fundamentalist Christians, even those often regarded as legalistic, have no objection to blood transfusions. Does the Watchtower Society possess unique insight, then, on medical matters?

To the contrary, the Society's track record calls for caution along these lines. The organization has changed its mind several times in the past on similar issues. For example, from the early 1930s onward, Jehovah's Witnesses were taught to refuse vaccinations, viewing them as a "direct violation" of God's law. (*Golden Age,* February 4, 1931, page 293) Two decades later that view was abandoned. In 1967 a decree came from Brooklyn headquarters ruling out organ transplants as a forbidden form of "cannibalism." (*The Watchtower,* November 15, 1967, pages 702–704) Thirteen years later that teaching was likewise discarded. In the meantime, some obedient members went blind rather than accept a cornea transplant. Others—including a JW elder who was a personal acquaintance of mine in Boston's nearby Hyde Park congregation—died rather than accept a kidney transplant. So, what assurance does a Witness have that the organization will not also reinterpret "God's law" on blood transfusions—perhaps after a loved one has died? The sect's track record on medical matters, when all the facts are known, does not inspire confidence.

Moreover, in interpreting certain verses to rule out blood transfusions, the Watchtower Society follows the pattern of the Jewish Pharisees who were noted for sticking to what appeared to be "the letter of the law" even when this proved harmful to their followers. When it came to the application of God's laws in life-threatening emergencies and situations involving human suffering, Jesus rebuked the Pharisees and declared that "the Sabbath was made to benefit man, and not man to benefit the Sabbath." (Mark 2:27 *Living Bible*) If a person, or even an animal, fell into a hole on the Sabbath, God would want people to do the necessary work—even if this appeared to break the Sabbath law—to pull him out, Jesus said. (Luke 14:5) He also went ahead and performed an act of healing on the Sabbath, in effect providing medical treatment the Pharisees saw as forbidden by God's law. (Mark 3:1–5; Luke 6:6–11)

The Pharisees were furious when Jesus healed the man's withered hand on the Sabbath. Similarly, a letter published in the December 8, 1984, issue of *The Concord Monitor* (New Hampshire) tells of Jehovah's Witness elders interrogating a terminal cancer patient in a hospital and then disfellowshipping him on his deathbed because he accepted a blood transfusion. We could easily picture the Pharisees doing the same thing—but would Jesus act like that?

Disturbing, too, is the Watchtower Society's official ruling that Jehovah's Witnesses may take certain components of blood, such as hemophiliac preparations (Factor VIII and Factor IX), immune globulins, and albumin, but that they must refuse other components such as white blood cells, plasma, red blood cells, and platelets. (June 22, 1982 *Awake!* magazine, pages 25–27) This is important because doctors nowadays administer such components more often than whole blood. According to other rulings discussed in the same article, JWs may even take whole blood that has merely circulated outside their body in a heart-lung machine, but may not store their own blood in advance of an operation. Nowhere to be found in Scripture, such artificial distinctions were decided arbitrarily by the sect's leadership, again reminiscent of the Pharisees.

Non-Witnesses who read the Bible itself find in it no command requiring that believers die rather than take blood transfusions. The millions of JWs who accept such an interpretation do so solely on the Watchtower Society's supposed authority—and would quickly reverse their position if and when the Society reverses its teaching. Clearly the Watchtower organization has gone "beyond the things that are written" (1 Corinthians 4:6 NWT) in interpreting biblical laws on animal sacrifice and kosher diet to prohibit the modern medical use of blood transfusions.

With what result? This doctrine does more than merely place the sect in the category of a "cult"; it also places large numbers of Jehovah's Witnesses in early graves. Dozens of JW deaths—names, places, dates, and other details—are documented in newspaper and magazine clippings I have personally collected in recent years. These clippings focus primarily on accident victims and minor children—cases brought to public attention through police or court intervention—but those dozens of deaths are a small fraction of the total that can be projected from available statistics.

The Watchtower itself has quoted statistics from published studies to the effect that refusing blood products adds "0.5% to 1.5% mortality to the overall operative risk" for JWs in routine surgery. (October 15, 1993, page 32) This means that one out of a hundred Witnesses undergoing routine surgery dies for lack of blood. One percent may be a small number in itself, but when applied to the roughly 12 million attending JW Kingdom Halls it translates into a large number—a cumulative death toll in the thousands for men, women, and children who live (and die!) by Watchtower law.

Born Again

Jesus told his secret visitor Nicodemus, "Verily, verily, I say unto thee, Except a man be born again, he cannot see the kingdom of God. . . . Except a man be born of water and of the Spirit, he cannot enter into the kingdom of God. . . . Marvel not that I said unto thee, Ye must be born again." (John 3:3–7) However, the Watchtower Society freely contradicts this, saying, "The 'other sheep' do not need any such rebirth, for their goal is life everlasting in the restored earthly paradise as subjects of the Kingdom." (The Watchtower, February 15, 1986, page 14)

The Society similarly disputes the testimony of churchgoers who claim to be born again. "Christendom's TV preachers lull millions into believing that they are 'saved' or 'born again.'" With these scornful words The Watchtower of April 1, 1988, introduces one of its unique teachings. "To whom does being 'born again' really apply?" The magazine explains that "a careful study of God's Word and Christ's teachings shows that only a limited number share the privilege of being born again," namely the 144,000 of Revelation 7:4 and 14:1–3. "The 'great crowd' of true Christians today do not need to be born again, since their hope of everlasting life is earthly, not heavenly." (page 18)

The Watchtower Society teaches that the evangelistic work Jesus assigned to his apostles would initially gather 144,000 true Christians who would rule with him from heaven, and that this number was completed in the year 1935. (*See* Heaven.) This total of 144,000 heaven-bound believers is supposedly made up of (1) thousands of first century Christians, (2) a smaller number of faithful men and women down through the centuries, and finally (3) the Watchtower faithful baptized prior to 1935. Evangelistic efforts from that year onward would be directed toward gathering a secondary class of believers, a "great crowd" (Revelation 7:9 NWT) or "great multitude, which no man could number" (KJV) who would be outside the new covenant Christian congregation but who would benefit from the new covenant much as the alien residents in ancient Israel benefited from the old covenant between God and the Jews. (*See* Great Crowd.) The New Testament, in this view, addresses its promises primarily to the 144,000—including what it says about being "born again."

Thus JWs believe that there are fewer than 9000 truly "born again" Christians alive on earth today, namely the remnant of elderly Witnesses baptized before 1935. The balance of the roughly 12 million attending JW Kingdom Halls as of this writing exclude themselves from this elite group. Naturally, then, they reject out of hand the thought that anyone outside the Watchtower organization might properly claim to be born again.

Are these beliefs solidly based on Scripture? Or do they derive from the imagination of the sect's leaders?

Paul writes in Romans 8:14–16 that "as many as are led by the Spirit of God, they are the sons of God . . . received the Spirit of adoption . . . are the children of God." (KJV) The JW *New World Translation*'s rendering agrees here with other modern English versions in saying that "all" who are led by God's Spirit receive this spiritual adoption or are reborn as God's children. "For all who are led by God's spirit, these are God's sons." (verse 14 NWT) What about those not in this category, those who have not received the Spirit of adoption? Do they form a secondary class of Christians? Far from it! Romans 8:9 says this concerning those not born of the Spirit: "if any man have not the Spirit of Christ, he is none of his" (KJV) or "if anyone does not have Christ's spirit, this one does not belong to him." (NWT) He is in "the flesh" rather than in the Spirit, and hence "cannot please God." (verse 8 KJV, NWT)

Scripture thus makes it clear that all who belong to Christ receive the Spirit of adoption; there is no secondary class of Christians who are not spirit-begotten as God's adopted children. One is either born again or not a Christian at all. Believers are automatically born again. As 1 John 5:1 says, "*Everyone* believing that Jesus is the Christ has been born from God." (NWT, emphasis added)

See also Heaven.

Censorship

On one occasion during the 1970s when I was still a Jehovah's Witness I called at the door of a religious man who insisted that he would accept my Watchtower literature only on the condition that I would also accept a magazine put out by his church. Today most Witnesses would automatically refuse such an offer. But at that time the instructions from headquarters were somewhat unclear, so, after some hesitation, I agreed—not that I had the slightest intention of looking open-mindedly at his material, but rather to give the appearance of being fair and reasonable, and to meet his condition for accepting Watchtower literature. After leaving his door I felt uncomfortable the rest of the day on account of the church magazine in my bookbag. And then, upon returning home, I left it in the car for fear that it might be inhabited by demons who might take up residence in my house if brought inside.

Looking back now at that incident, I realize that my response was far from typical of Jehovah's Witnesses. I was not more fearful than most; on the contrary, I was less fearful. Most Witnesses would never have accepted the church magazine in the first place.

Since the 1970s ended, the Watchtower Society has clarified the issue for its followers by strongly cautioning them against reading outside material, especially pieces written by former members, whom it refers to as "apostates." Since I fall into that category myself, my books are greatly feared by JWs. One non-Witness man who purchased a couple of my books in the hope of rescuing his wife from the sect made the mistake of letting her see the books; fearful that he had brought demons into the house, she spent many sleepless nights and was tormented by nightmares when she did manage to doze off.

So, Christians evangelizing Jehovah's Witnesses need to be aware of their attitude toward Christian literature: the material most likely to help them is viewed as off-limits and potentially harmful. How, then, can such material be used in winning them to Christ? And, how can the barrier be broken down so that a JW will read literature addressing his needs? The answers to these questions can best be understood after looking more deeply into the matter.

First it should be noted that the publications of the Watch Tower Bible and Tract Society are currently under government ban in certain lands. Persons found distributing or even possessing the Society's literature in those jurisdictions face possible arrest and imprisonment. For the most part such restrictions exist today only in totalitarian countries that also restrict other literature—countries where freedom of the press is a foreign concept. Surprisingly, though, even the Western democracies have, at one time or another, placed restrictions on the publications of Jehovah's Witnesses—or Russellite "Bible Students" as they were formerly known. For example, a ban was imposed in Canada during both world wars, and several of the sect's leaders received 20-year prison sentences in the United States during World War I in connection with allegedly "seditious" passages in the Society's periodicals and in its book *The Finished Mystery*.

In view of such a history, one would expect Jehovah's Witnesses to be especially sensitive to the issue of freedom of the press. And they are—when it involves distribution of *their* literature. Thus the October 22, 1987, *Awake!* magazine commends the U.S. Supreme Court for upholding the Witnesses' "privilege of freely disseminating religious teachings by the printed page" during the second world war (page 26) and applauds the Court for saying "freedom to differ is not limited to things that do not matter much. That would be a mere shadow of freedom. The test of its substance is the right to differ as to things that touch the heart of the existing order." (page 27)

What happens, though, when an individual Jehovah's Witness writes, publishes, or distributes material that Watchtower leaders do not approve of? Then the Society takes a different approach to the matter of freedom of the press. As editor of the quarterly *Comments from the Friends,* I can testify to that personally: I was put on trial by a Watchtower "judicial committee" early in 1982 for publishing the first two issues. At that point I was still a Jehovah's Witness in good standing. My writings did not make any radical departure from Watchtower teachings on doctrinal matters but did challenge the elevation of the Society itself to a position of near-papal authority. How did the Society respond? Late one night when my wife and I were returning home from a Bible study, two elders stepped out of a parked car and accosted us in the darkness on the sidewalk in front of our home. They demanded to know whether I planned to publish another issue. I asked them what they objected to in the first two issues, but they insisted that they could not discuss content, since they had been sent simply to find out if I planned to keep publishing. When I answered in the affirmative, they turned and left. A few days later a "judicial committee" tried us in absentia and disfellowshipped us.

Lest anyone assume that this was the high-handed action of a few local elders, it should be pointed out that these men were in communication with Brooklyn headquarters over my situation. Moreover, the Society has since laid down firm guidelines to prevent followers from circulating or possessing unauthorized literature. The May 1, 1984, *Watchtower*, under the heading "Questions from Readers" on page 31, asks this loaded question: "Why do Jehovah's Witnesses decline to exchange their Bible study aids for the religious literature of people they meet?" The official answer states, in part, that

> it would be foolhardy, as well as a waste of valuable time, for Jehovah's Witnesses to accept and expose themselves to false religious literature that is designed to deceive. . . . Hence, it is out of wisdom and respect for God's counsel that Jehovah's Witnesses do not make a practice of exchanging valuable Bible study aids containing Scriptural truth for religious literature that disseminates error or apostate views.

Rather than put in print some even stronger warnings that smack of religious totalitarianism, the Society usually leaves it up to circuit and district overseers to counsel Witnesses not to read literature from outside the organization. However, the March 15, 1986, *Watchtower* actually features a photo of a woman tossing mail into the trash before the postman has left the property, with the caption, "Do you wisely destroy apostate material?" (page 12) The article goes on to ask, "Why is reading apostate publications similar to reading pornographic literature?" (page 14), and warns JWs to "beware of those who try to put forward their own contrary opinions." (page 17)

The November 1, 1987, *Watchtower* bemoans the fact that some Witnesses "have exposed themselves to possible spiritual contamination by tuning in to religious radio and television broadcasts." (page 19) And this article goes on to say that "False religious propaganda from any source should be avoided like poison! Really, since our Lord has used 'the faithful and discreet slave' to convey to us 'sayings of everlasting life,' why should we ever want to look anywhere else?" (page 20)

The September 1987 issue of *Our Kingdom Ministry*, an instructional newsletter circulated only to active Witnesses, goes beyond the area of religious writings by cautioning JWs not "to circulate among the brothers private material on matters such as medical or counseling services." (page 4)

Watchtower leaders freely use the punishment of shunning to isolate troublesome writers and those who dare read their writings. Thus, active Witnesses who subscribe to my quarterly *Comments from the Friends* must do so secretly to avoid being cut off from family and friends. Some have it mailed to them at their place of employment or in care of a neighbor. Others rent a post office box and use an assumed name, initials, or simply "boxholder."

One active JW in the Midwest related to me in a letter how he regularly smuggled his copy of *Comments from the Friends* into his place of secular employment and made several photocopies of the entire publication. (His boss, also a Witness, had given him permission to use the Xerox for personal papers, never imagining that he would be reprinting forbidden literature.) Then he would take the seven or eight copies with him to Kingdom Hall, where he would surreptitiously distribute them to a number of other local Witnesses.

The book *Crisis of Conscience* by ex-Governing Body member Raymond Franz also circulates underground among dissident Witnesses. One told how he tore the cover off the book before reading it, so that it would be more difficult to identify in case someone might observe him.

All of this should make it obvious to thinking Witnesses that their leaders have something to hide—certain facts that they don't want followers to discover. And, indeed, although virtually all JWs will recite the official "party line" in the presence of others, some entertain doubts and, if certain that no one is watching them, will cautiously look into forbidden writings.

They will not do this, of course, in the presence of another Witness who might feel obligated to report them to the elders. They are also unlikely to accept opposing literature from the hand of someone they know personally, or someone they have been preaching to, for fear that such a move would betray their own inward doubts and thus spoil their efforts to convert the other party.

In view of all this, the best way to get Christian literature into the hands of a JW you know personally would be through a discreet third party when the Witness is not in the company of others, or anonymously through the mail if it can be guaranteed that another family member will not open the package or become suspicious.

If, on the other hand, the Witness you desire to reach is a stranger calling at the door, a couple of approaches could be used: Occasionally a JW calling alone will ignore instructions from headquarters and accept material in exchange for the literature he is offering—but this is rare. Alternatively, you might be able to get him or her to read a Christian tract if you start out this way: "I was hoping a Jehovah's Witness would call. I saved this piece of literature so that I could ask the next Witness I met to check it out. Can you tell me if it is correct or not in what it is saying?"

The most successful approach is usually to document the sect's false prophecies and other erroneous teachings by showing them photocopies from their own literature. Before you meet with the Witnesses, thumb through my book *How to Rescue Your Loved One from the Watchtower,* or another book with full-page reproductions from Watchtower Society books and magazines that will prove your point. Photocopy the pages, and cut off any added material at the top or bottom of the page, leaving only the original Watchtower material. Then say to the Witness:

"Surely you don't object to looking at your own publications. This is a copy of page (number) of your book (title of book). Notice what the underlined portion says." Then proceed with your discussion, or turn to another photocopy for more proof. Be prepared for the possibility that the Witness may suspect that you or your source tampered with the copy, altering the words to produce false evidence against the organization. He or she may want to take the photocopy home or to Kingdom Hall to compare it with the original and verify the wording.

Even when it comes to their own materials—whether photocopies or the originals, your approach and presentation may determine whether or not the Jehovah's Witness will look at the evidence you produce. If you begin by arguing, denouncing the Watchtower, or expressing your intention to get the Witness out of the organization, he or she may feel obligated not to cooperate at all, not even by looking at Watchtower materials from your hand. Or if the Witness fears that you have joined forces with "apostates" the door may be closed to any further discussions.

It is usually best to proceed as dispassionately as possible, letting the facts speak for themselves rather than trying to impose your personal conclusions or judgments on the Witness. For example, instead of saying, "Look at this documentary proof that the Watchtower is a false prophet and a liar!" you will get much further by saying something like this: "Because of my interest in your organization I've gone to the library and to bookstores to research beyond the magazines you gave me, and I've found a lot of other material—both Watchtower publications and outside sources. I was left with a few questions, though. Could you please help me answer my questions? They relate to things I read on these pages from Watchtower publications that I've photocopied."

Telling a Jehovah's Witness that his organization is a false prophet merely makes him angry and defensive. He believes that your assertion must be a false accusation. But if you—in a non-threatening way—get him to read actual Watchtower predictions for the years 1914, 1925, 1975, etc., all of which failed to come true, he will be forced to conclude for himself that the group prophesied falsely.

Moreover, by approaching a JW with questions rather than with accusations, you are working with his mental programming rather than against it. He is trained to walk away from criticism of the organization, refusing even to listen. But he is trained to come to the aid of people who have questions, confident that he has all the answers. It takes self-discipline on the part of a Christian to use this approach, holding back from denouncing the sect while calmly presenting the evidence, but the superior results are worth the effort.

Of course, once a Jehovah's Witness has reviewed the evidence and has begun to express doubts about the sect, then it is possible to go beyond Watchtower photocopies and to begin directing him or her to outside reading materials. The best place to start is with publications written specifically for JWs by ex-JWs. The reason for this is that even those members who have begun to think for themselves and who are thinking of leaving the group are still heavily influenced in their thinking by the indoctrination they have received over the years. They may be starting to explore the outside world, but they are doing so with a JW mind-set and with certain assumptions unique to the sect. Written material, to be most effective, should meet them on common ground and gently expand their horizons.

To grasp the importance of taking their feelings into consideration when selecting reading materials, consider the different approaches the Apostle Paul used when addressing different audiences. He won over Jewish Pharisees by immediately identifying himself as "the son of a Pharisee" and declaring "the hope and resurrection of the dead." (Acts 23:6 KJV) But, when speaking to Greeks in Athens, he established common ground by introducing his message this way: "Men of Athens! I see that in every way you are very religious. For as I walked around and observed your objects of worship, I even found an altar with this inscription: TO AN UNKNOWN GOD. Now what you worship as something unknown I am going to proclaim to you." (Acts 17:22–23 NIV) Had he started out telling the Greeks about being a Pharisee and about the resurrection, he would not have gotten very far; nor would he have made progress if he had begun talking to the Pharisees about an idolatrous altar. But in each case he knew how to approach his audience in the manner necessary to meet them where they were.

With these thoughts in mind, the book that many who are leaving the Witnesses find easiest to read first and most helpful at that stage of their thinking is *Crisis of Conscience* by Raymond V. Franz (Commentary Press, Atlanta, 1983). Nephew of Watchtower President Frederick W. Franz, and a former member himself of the organization's Governing Body, Raymond Franz provides insight into the sect's inner secrets that JWs find fascinating. Avoiding doctrinal issues, Franz focuses on the organization itself, exposing the myth that it is divinely directed by revealing the role personalities and political infighting played in leadership decisions. The book helps readers deprogram themselves of the notion that it is "God's organization" and to see the Watchtower instead as a pretentious human institution.

A next step for many who exit the group is to read my book *Jehovah's Witnesses Answered Verse by Verse* (Baker Book House, 1986). One local couple told me that they stayed up an entire night reading it together and looking up the Scripture references, with the result that many problem issues were cleared up for them. The next week they came to our support group for the first time and attended church with us the following Sunday.

After this sort of foundational reading, it is possible for the new ex-JW to branch out into a broader range of literature.

Channel of Communication

"Unless we are in touch with this channel of communication that God is using, we will not progress along the road to life, no matter how much Bible reading we do." That official pronouncement in *The Watchtower* magazine of December 1, 1981 (page 27) enunciates the single most important doctrine of Jehovah's Witnesses, namely their belief that people today can have a relationship with God *only* through the Watchtower organization. If you are not "in touch with this channel of communication that God is using," your Bible reading is useless, your prayer is pointless, and your fellowship with other believers is a waste of time. You can progress along the road to everlasting life in God's kingdom *only* by listening obediently to the Watchtower Society's Brooklyn headquarters.

This is the most important JW doctrine, because all the other teachings of the sect depend on this one. In fact, all of the other doctrines are subject to change whenever the "channel of communication" sees fit to change them. At various times the Watchtower organization has expressed various doctrinal flip-flops: it has promoted Christmas and attacked Christmas; presented Christ as almighty and denied that Christ is almighty; attributed the Great Pyramid to God and attributed it to Satan; banned organ transplants and recommended organ transplants, and so on. The only doctrine that never changes is the organization's claim to speak for God on all these matters: "It is vital that we . . . respond to the directions of the 'slave' as we would to the voice of God." (*The Watchtower*, June 15, 1957, page 370. *See* Faithful and Discreet Slave.)

Failure to understand this fact is what often leaves Christians banging their heads against a stone wall, so to speak, when discussing doctrine with a Witness. The Christian presents a biblical argument on the subject of deity or the afterlife, in the hope of giving the JW a different doctrinal understanding. The JW listens but remains unaffected by the evidence. Why? Because the JW's beliefs are based not on evidence or logic but on the *authority* of the Watchtower Society. This fact is demonstrated whenever the leadership does a turnabout on a doctrinal issue: the new interpretation is published in *The Watchtower* magazine, and millions of Jehovah's Witnesses simultaneously change their mind as to what to believe. I saw this happen many times during my thirteen years in the organization. A Christian may have been arguing the very same point with a Witness the week before with no effect, but as soon as it is published in the pages of *The Watchtower* the Witness believes it.

So, trying to prove the deity of Christ or the personality of the Holy Spirit while a JW still sees the Watchtower Society as God's "channel of communication" is like trying to put the cart before the horse. Usually, it won't work. The Watchtower's authority is the driving force behind the JW's doctrinal thinking, and the JW must be disconnected from that driving force before he or she can be led off in another direction.

Before other issues can be addressed successfully, it is usually necessary first to disprove this central doctrine that serves as a foundation for all the others. Once you disprove the Society's claim to be God's spokesman, you undermine all the other doctrines the Society teaches in God's name. They can then be addressed individually on their own merits.

How, then, is it possible to awaken a follower to the fact that the Watchtower Society is not really God's channel? The most effective way to accomplish this is to get him or her to examine closely the very things "communicated" over the years in God's name: the failed prophecies, doctrinal flip-flops, and dishonest deceptions that characterize communications as coming from man rather than from God. (*See* Beth-Sarim, Higher Powers, Organ Transplants, Pleiades, and many other topics discussed in this book.) Once the JW realizes that the Brooklyn organization has spoken with man's confused voice in these obvious instances, it will become apparent that the more abstract theological teachings as well originate from this unreliable source rather than from "the voice of God."

See also Faithful and Discreet Slave *and* God's Organization.

Child Custody

Verbal debates with Jehovah's Witnesses are not limited to doorstep encounters or efforts to evangelize a JW relative or workmate; today's high divorce rate often sees the discussion move to the courtroom when there is a custody fight over minor children with religiously divided parents. On Sunday evening, December 29, 1992, millions of TV viewers got a glimpse of this. The CBS network program "Sixty Minutes" devoted a segment to the David-*versus-*

Goliath aspect that such legal battles take on when a non-Witness mate pays out-of-pocket for a local general-practice lawyer while the Watchtower Society mobilizes its experienced legal department to provide free assistance to the JW party. This may involve flying in expert New York attorneys armed with reams of case law and other materials to offer in evidence.

Arguments in such cases generally focus on fears that a child in custody of a JW parent would not receive a needed blood transfusion in the event of accident or illness (see Blood Transfusions), would be deprived of a college education (see Education), would lose contact with non JW relatives (see Shunning), or would be emotionally harmed or socially disadvantaged by other cultic teachings.

Jehovah's Witness youngsters are taught that door-to-door service and Kingdom Hall activities should be "the most important thing in their lives"—The Watchtower, April 1, 1979, page 14. The organization's 1983 booklet School and Jehovah's Witnesses spells out policies restricting youngsters from participation in school dances, elective offices, holiday celebrations, sex education classes, flag ceremonies, the singing or playing of patriotic or religious music, and organized sports. For example:

"Witness parents encourage their children to use after-school hours principally to pursue spiritual interests, rather than to excel in some sport. Participation in organized sports, we believe, would expose Witness youths to unwholesome associations."
—School and Jehovah's Witnesses, page 23

Yet, when custody cases go to court and such aspects of JW child rearing are brought up as an issue, a booklet prepared by the Watchtower legal department instructs youngsters to testify to the exact opposite of what they would say if speaking to a Witness audience:

> "Be careful that they don't get the impression that they are in a demonstration at the circuit assembly, when they would show that the first things in life are service and going to the Kingdom Hall. Show hobbies, crafts, social activity, sports, and especially plans for the future. Be careful they don't all say that they are going to be pioneers. Plans can be trade, getting married and having children, journalism, and all kinds of other things. Maybe you can show an interest in art and the theatre . . . interests that you would expect from other young people."
>
> —Direct and Cross-Examination Questions in Child Custody Cases, page 42; Preparing for Child Custody Cases, page 43

Here the Society acknowledges that it is instructing youngsters to testify in court to something different from what they would say "at the circuit assembly" to a Witness audience. This requires them to engage in a form of double-talk that most people would consider lying. Unless the youngsters are to see themselves as liars, they must also engage in double-think, the mental gymnastics described in George Orwell's novel *Nineteen Eighty-Four,* where people are forced by a totalitarian society "to be conscious of complete truthfulness while telling carefully constructed lies"—*Nineteen Eighty-Four,* page 32.

Personally, I know of only four attorneys nationwide with expertise in matters pertaining to Jehovah's Witnesses, and I believe that only one of them routinely gets involved with custody cases. Not practicing law in every state, the best they can usually do is consult with a local attorney actually handling a case. Christian counter-cult ministries have privately published only a small amount of material aimed at refuting the arguments Watchtower lawyers use in court. Still, cases can be won, especially when the JW parent takes an extreme position endangering the health or emotional well-being of a child.

A word of caution is in order, however, for Christians called to the aid of someone battling a Jehovah's Witness mate in court. First of all, care should be taken not to establish legal precedents that could backfire against the Christian community. Secular courts may view a Christian refusing to okay an abortion for a wayward teenage daughter the same way they would view a JW parent denying a child a blood transfusion. Moreover, just as the Watchtower Society is wrong to conclude that the Witness is automatically the better parent and the one deserving custody, the converse should also be recognized: namely, that someone fighting a JW mate is not thereby automatically the better parent, either. In some cases discerning the best interests of the child may involve identifying the lesser of two evils. That was true of the case King Solomon settled at 1 Kings 3:16–28 where the two women laying claim to a baby boy were both harlots.

God says, "I hate divorce" (Malachi 2:16), and anyone observing a child custody battle can understand why. No matter which party wins, the children usually lose. A far better goal is to put the marriage back together and to keep the family intact. Those who say that this cannot be done with one mate a JW are either ignorant of the facts or motivated by other factors. One man who contacted me in 1989, looking for referral to a lawyer so that he could divorce his JW wife and take custody of their eight youngsters, took my advice instead, remained with her, and tells me now how proud he is of the older children they have finished raising together—and that he and his wife now enjoy a closer relationship than ever before. I could name a number of such religiously mixed couples who are making a success of it. The key seems to be love *and respect* for one another and love for the children. This enables couples to focus on the areas of agreement rather than their differences.

If the Christian mate and the JW mate are sincere in their respective beliefs, both can work at applying the marriage-healing counsel of 1 Peter, chapter 3. Moreover, even when things do not go smoothly, both can apply to themselves Paul's words at 1 Corinthians 7:11–14:

> ... If any brother has a wife who is not a believer and she is willing to live with him, he must not divorce her. And if a woman has a husband who is not a believer and he is willing to live with her, she must not divorce him. For the unbelieving husband has been sanctified through his wife, and the unbelieving wife has been sanctified through her believing husband. Otherwise your children would be unclean, but as it is, they are holy. (NIV)

Christ

Jehovah's Witnesses agree that Jesus is the Christ or Messiah, meaning *anointed one*, but they attach such a narrow definition to the term that they miss much of its significance. *The Watchtower* declares that "Jesus could not bear the title 'Christ' until he was anointed by Jehovah's spirit at the time of his baptism in 29 C.E." (January 1, 1969, page 29) It stresses this limited application of the title "Christ" because JW leaders view Jesus Christ as an earthly manifestation of Michael the Archangel, a mere created being who was given the assignment of fulfilling the role of Christ among men on earth.

The Bible, on the other hand, presents Jesus Christ as timeless: "Jesus Christ the same yesterday, and to day, and for ever." (Hebrews 13:8) He is "the Lamb slain from the foundation of the world." (Revelation 13:8)

Since the angels, of course, know the timeless Christ of the Bible rather than the limited Christ of the Watchtower, it was no problem for the angel to call him "Christ" at the time of his birth, when announcement was made to the shepherds near Bethlehem: "There was born to you today a Savior, who is Christ the Lord." (Luke 2:11 NWT)

See also our chapters "Jesus Christ" and "Michael the Archangel."

Christendom

Jehovah's Witnesses describe themselves as the only "true followers of Christ," totally separate from "Christendom's religions." (*Mankind's Search for God*, page 346) However, in order to place themselves outside of Christendom, they must redefine the word.

Dictionaries typically define *Christendom* as "1. Christian lands. 2. Christians collectively." or as "1. Christians collectively. 2. the Christian world." (*Funk & Wagnalls Standard Desk Dictionary*, 1983, and *The American College Dictionary*, 1963) The same dictionaries define *Jehovah's Witnesses* as "A Christian sect . . ." or as "a sect of Christians . . ." So, according to the standard dictionary definitions, Jehovah's Witnesses are a sect of Christendom.

Of course, problems result whenever the same word means different things to different people. An American visiting England who steps urgently into his host's *bathroom* will be disappointed to find no toilet there, since the British use the word *bathroom* to designate a room set aside for bathing. The American should ask for the *water closet*. Similarly, a judge with a prison inmate appearing before him will be unprepared for the violent rage he may provoke by calling him a *punk*. Although the judge means "a petty hoodlum," in prison lingo a *punk* means one who regularly submits to sodomy.

Such misunderstandings, in most cases, do not happen by design; words slowly develop different meanings in different cultural settings. In the case of Jehovah's Witnesses, however, there may be something more involved. Authorities on "brainwashing" or mind control list "loaded language" among the instruments used by cult leaders to control the thinking of their followers. Steven Hassan, a professional exit counselor and former member of the Unification Church ["Moonies"], writes

> The cult's "loaded language" had created little cubbyholes in my mind, and when I was a member, all reality was filtered through them. The faster an ex-member reclaims words and their real meaning, the faster his recovery.
> —*Combatting Cult Mind Control* by Steven Hassan
> (Park Street Press, 1988) page 176

The Watchtower Society's redefinition of the word *Christendom* to include all *other* nominally Christian groups, but *not* itself, is a perfect example of such "loaded language." It is just one small part of a subtle mind control program.

According to the real dictionary definition of the word, Jehovah's Witnesses are indeed a sect of Christendom. And this is neither a mere technicality nor a matter of definition only; both theologically and historically Jehovah's Witnesses fall within the boundaries of Christendom. Their similar doctrines place them in among such groups as the Christadelphians, certain Adventists, the late Herbert Armstrong's Worldwide Church of God, the Laymen's Home Missionary Movement, and numerous Russellite "Bible Student" fellowships.

Moreover, the historical roots of Jehovah's Witnesses tie them in as a sect closely related to those just named. Through his predictions that Christ would return in 1843 or 1844 Baptist lay preacher William Miller led thousands from Baptist and other mainline churches into a new religious movement. Following their disappointment when Christ failed to appear, Miller's followers regrouped into several sects under the broad heading of "Adventism" including the Advent Christian Church and the better-known Seventh-Day Adventists. Watchtower founder Charles Taze Russell began attending Adventist religious services as a teenage boy in the late 1860s and remained under the teaching of various Adventist mentors for some ten years before starting his own sect in 1879 with a nucleus of fellow-believers:

> Looking back to 1871, we see that many of our company were what are known as Second Adventists, and the light they held briefly stated, was that there would be a second advent of Jesus . . . in 1873, because the 6,000 years from the creation of Adam were complete then.
> —*Zion's Watch Tower*, February 1881, page 3

Russell's followers, in turn, split up after his death to form several sects, including the one that Joseph Rutherford renamed Jehovah's Witnesses in 1931 to distinguish it from the others.

Historically, then, Jehovah's Witnesses arose within Christendom, and doctrinally they remain an Adventist sect of Christendom, albeit an heretical one.

See Adventist Origins.

Christmas

". . . those who celebrate Christmas do not honor God or Christ, but honor pagan celebrations and pagan gods." This declaration in an *Awake!* magazine of December 8, 1988 (page 19) sums up the Watchtower Society's teaching on the holiday—a teaching that the Society's magazines reemphasize each December lest some of the flock forget and erroneously conclude 'tis the season to be jolly.

Criticism of Christmas in those articles focuses first of all on the date. Religious and secular sources are quoted to establish the well-known fact that the actual date of the

Savior's birth is unknown. The articles then attack selection of December 25th as an arbitrary date to celebrate the event, because pagans were already holding winter festivals on that date. The implication is that the Church did not try to supplant the pagan festival with a Christian one, but rather that the Church merely attached a new name to the old holiday so that believers could join in.

JW articles go on to trace the Christmas tree to pagan worship; they focus on greed and commercialism that surfaces during the Christmas shopping season; they point out that the holiday is celebrated in oriental lands where the general population makes no pretense of being believers in Christ.

From all of this they argue that Christmas is a pagan holiday inappropriate for Christians to share in.

Interestingly, however, *The Watchtower* did not always express this viewpoint. The organization's founders and early leaders celebrated Christmas and encouraged others to do the same:

> "Christmas Day," in celebration of our dear Redeemer's birth, has for long centuries been celebrated on December 25th; and although it is now well known that this date is in error, and that it more properly corresponds with the date of the annunciation to Mary, nine months before our Lord was born, and that he was born about October 1st,— nevertheless, since the Lord has given no instructions whatever upon this subject, and since it is proper to do good deeds and think good thoughts upon any day, it cannot be improper, in harmony with general usage, for us to remember in a social way our dear Redeemer's birth at this time.
> —*Zion's Watch Tower*, December 15, 1898, page 370

> It matters not particularly that December 25 is not the anniversary of our Lord's birth, according to the Scriptural account; that really he was born about September 25, nine

months later. One day, as well as another, will serve us to commemorate our Savior's birth in the flesh, as a gift of God's love to a condemned and dying world.

—*Zion's Watch Tower,* December 15, 1908, page 379

The early Watchtower leaders who felt this way were just as familiar as today's leaders with the resemblance between pagan customs and certain Christmas traditions. They welcomed opportunities to share with others in honoring Christ, while today's leaders seem more eager to keep followers separated from non-JW relatives and neighbors. (Some form of isolation from outsiders is a common thread found in many mind-control cults. With some groups this separation is accomplished by physically withdrawing into a commune, while in other cults members continue living in the outside world but withdraw from social contact with non-members.)

Participation in Christmas celebrations is not optional for Jehovah's Witnesses. The ban is enforced by elders who make up judicial committees that sit in judgment of any who celebrate the holiday, even in some small way. During my 8 years as a JW elder I took part in such enforcement proceedings on a number of occasions. I recall that we elders even summoned for discipline a newly-married young man whose non-Witness wife hung an evergreen wreath on their apartment door. We told him that he had to take down the decoration or face punishment since God held him responsible as head of the house.

Discussions between Christians and Jehovah's Witnesses on this subject are often hampered by strong emotions that come into play on both sides. Understandably, believers in Christ who hold the holiday dear as His special day may have trouble communicating with JWs who feel just as strongly that it is a satanic mockery. It proves helpful, therefore, to promote reasonableness and to seek common ground. Show appreciation for the Witness's sincerity and desire to please God. You might even want to make it clear that you yourself strongly disapprove of the "celebrating" some people do such as getting drunk at office parties or flirting with other's mates under mistletoe.

Explain that there are really *two different celebrations* taking place on December 25th: One is the festival promoted by department stores and liquor companies and celebrated even by non-Christians in pagan lands. Its central figure is Santa Claus, and its main focus is on having a "good time." The other is the commemoration of the birth of Jesus Christ by sincere Christians.

"And many will rejoice over his birth," said the angel concerning the birth of John the Baptist six months before Jesus. (Luke 1:14 in the JW *New World Translation*) How much more so, then, is the birth of our Savior a cause for rejoicing! Christians use the day to honor Chris̄ by gathering to sing hymns, to pray, and to praise the Lord, while non-believers see it as an occasion to party.

Trying to convince a Jehovah's Witness that *he* or *she* ought to celebrate the holiday is an unrealistic approach. There are enough other obstacles—organizational discipline and peer rejection, for example—to make such an accomplishment virtually impossible, at least in the course of a single discussion. A better goal would be to get the Witness to stop judging *you* for celebrating.

Appeal to the JW not to blame you for other people's over-indulgence in food and drink, or for their greedy commercialization of a day you hold sacred. Ask the Witness if he can rightly condemn you for honoring Christ on that day, in view of what Paul wrote concerning the Roman Christians and Jewish holidays: "One man esteemeth one day above another: another esteemeth every day [alike]. Let every man be fully persuaded in his own mind. He that regardeth the day, regardeth [it] unto the Lord." (Romans 14:5–6)

See also Holidays *and* Birthdays.

Chronology

The study of the sequence and dating of biblical events plays a dual role in the beliefs of Jehovah's Witnesses. First, it provides convincing evidence that the Watchtower Society is God's organization. (Who else on earth today has such a clear grasp of God's past, present, and future dealings, all the way from Adam to Armageddon?) Second, it underpins the endtimes prophecies promoted by the sect. (When biblical scholarship uncovers the dates in God's biblical appointment calendar for Christ's Second Coming and the Rapture, who can question dates set by God himself?)

I recall clearly the powerful impact that chronological arguments in Watchtower literature had on my mind when I first encountered the sect as a young man in my early twenties. Since the age of fourteen I had been a confirmed atheist. For some years my college studies and extracurricular reading had focused on science, mathematics, history, and humanistic philosophy. I prided myself on being a skeptic's skeptic—certainly not a candidate for blind faith in any sort of religious mysticism. I laughed at Christian invitations to "believe and be saved," but the JW challenge to "study" intrigued me—especially when the Watchtower books I opened in 1968 presented biblical stories, not as matters of blind faith, but as documented events precisely pinpointed on a time line stretching from the creation of Adam in 4026 B.C. to the end of Christ's Millennial Reign in the year 2975 A.D. Would God really wipe out corrupt human governments in 1975 and install Christ as king around October 4th or 5th of that year? The Witnesses I spoke with never asked me to accept anything on faith; they invited me to study the evidence. I accepted the invitation, was duly impressed, and soon found myself joining the sect.

The JW approach starts out with detailed dating of biblical events through calculations employing time periods found in Scripture: the ages of kings and patriarchs when they died and when their sons were born; the numbers of years that various kings and judges ruled in Israel and Judah; and the occasional passages of Scripture that speak of longer time spans. Next, the Witnesses focus on events that are mentioned in both biblical and secular history, such as the start of John the Baptist's preaching career "in the fifteenth year of Tiberius Caesar" (Luke 3:1) or Nehemiah's petition in "the month of Nisan in the twentieth year of King Artaxerxes" of Persia. (Nehemiah 2:1 NIV) They then use the calendar dates of the secular references to calculate the calendar dates of all the other biblical events.

At this point, when their students have been both bored and overwhelmed by scores of pages and seemingly endless hours of kings and calculations—when the students are saying, "Okay, okay, I believe you; I don't need to go through the calculations myself"—the Witnesses go on to discuss the Gentile Times of Luke 21:24 as evidence that Christ returned invisibly 2520 years after 607 B.C., shortly after the start of World War I in 1914. (*See* Appointed Times of the Nations.) To this they add Christ's words that "this generation shall not pass, till all these things be fulfilled" (Matthew 24:34) and they come up with "the Creator's promise of a peaceful and secure new world before the generation that saw the events of 1914 passes away." (*Awake!*, February 8, 1995, page 4)*

How can Christians respond to a JW or to one of their prospective converts who is awed by the Watchtower Society's chronological articles? Perhaps the first response should be to acquaint the individual with some of the chronological writings produced by orthodox Christians.

---

*As this book was going to press, the Watchtower Society dropped this statement from the *Awake!* magazine's masthead. (*See* False Prophets, *footnote*.)

The people who are greatly impressed by the Watchtower material are usually those who have done little or no prior reading on the subject and who are therefore unaware of the extensive literature on Bible chronology available in church libraries and through Christian bookstores. Even a cursory look at the volumes generated by writers associated with orthodox denominations will reveal the Watchtower's efforts to be small in comparison. A closer look will reveal that the JW writers lack academic credentials, that they have done little or no original research, and that they have borrowed most of their material from non-Witness sources.

A characteristic difference is that chronological works found in church libraries and Christian bookstores often mention historical uncertainties and differences of opinion among scholars, whereas the JW articles tend to be one-sided and dogmatic. Questions that cannot be resolved by examination of available facts are resolved in the Watchtower writings by an arbitrary decree of the leadership.

After pointing out that traditional Christians have outdone the Witnesses in terms of original chronological research and in terms of sheer volume of material produced, you can draw attention to two major flaws found throughout the JW writings. First, they have given rise over the years to numerous failed prophecies. (*See* False Prophecies.) Second, the Watchtower articles demonstrate narrow self-centeredness to an amazing degree.

In an example of the latter, the Society's second president Joseph F. Rutherford wrote that *he* was God's chosen instrument for disclosing to mankind the seven seals of Revelation chapters 5–8, that the seven angelic trumpet blasts in Revelation chapters 8–11 foretold resolutions *he* presented to conventions held between 1922 and 1928, and that the pouring out of the seven bowls of God's wrath in Revelation chapter 16 foretold proclamations *he* presented at Witness conventions. (See his book *Light*, Vol. 1, pages 72–73 and 105–227; Vol. 2, pages 19–60.) The Watchtower Society today still teaches that the Bible foretold specific events in the lives of Rutherford and his associates. Thus, the November 1, 1993, *Watchtower* (pages 11–12) applies the 1260 days, 1290 days, and 1335 days of Daniel 12:7, 11–12 to the date Rutherford was sentenced to prison, the date he spoke at a convention in Ohio, and the date a book he wrote was released to the public. Such absurdities are sufficient to alert outsiders to the specious nature of Watchtower chronologies, and even some Jehovah's Witnesses who read them will blush with embarrassment.

See also Appointed Times of the Nations.

Church/Churches

To a well-indoctrinated Jehovah's Witness the Watchtower organization is the one true Church. So, all the other churches that claim to be Christian appear as impostors, counterfeits created by Satan the devil. And the very fact that there are many such church bodies is offered as proof that this is so.

"Look at all the different churches!" Jehovah's Witnesses say. "They all disagree with each other—Baptists, Mormons, Catholics, Pentecostals, and so on. In contrast to the many churches of Christendom, we Jehovah's Witnesses form just one organization and have unity among ourselves."

To demonstrate that this argument is a fallacious one, simply substitute for "Jehovah's Witnesses" the name of some other tight-knit religious group. For example, one could say, "We Mormons have the truth. Look at all the different churches! They all disagree with each other—Baptists, Jehovah's Witnesses, Catholics, Pentecostals, and so on. In contrast with the many churches of Christendom, we Mormons form just one organization and have unity among ourselves."

Several other sects do indeed use this very argument to "prove" that their particular organization is God's one Church—in contrast to all the others which are divided among themselves. But the error in logic is that anyone can limit their own group to persons who are in total agreement, and then point to the divisions in the rest of the world. Choosing to see things from only one narrow perspective, the members of such a group fall for the "us-against-them" argument without realizing that it is a logical fallacy used by other cults as well.

If an individual Jehovah's Witness were able to step back for a moment and view the whole religious scene objectively, he or she would see that the Watchtower organization fits into its own niche in a diverse spectrum of nominally "Christian" groups espousing a wide range of beliefs. While JWs differ greatly from those at another end of the spectrum, such as Greek Orthodox or Roman Catholic, the Witnesses are actually quite similar to certain other groups of the same religious "family" as themselves. In fact, JWs are so similar to Russellite Bible Students, certain Adventists, and the Worldwide Church of God, that many outsiders find it difficult to tell them apart. However, like a certain group of Hassidic Jews who were reported in the news as battling another group of Hassidic Jews that differed from them only on the question of whether to turn the brim of their black hats up or down, Jehovah's Witnesses feel the greatest hostility toward those who are closest to them, yet not part of their group.

Thus, they refuse to see themselves as related to the Adventists, although it is a well-documented fact that their founder C. T. Russell edited an Adventist magazine before leading several other Adventists to break away over just one or two issues of disagreement and start publishing *Zion's Watch Tower*. (For additional details, *see* Adventist

81

Origins.) JWs also hold the worst possible opinion of groups that, in turn, broke away from the Watchtower Society in years past—also often over minor issues or personalities—even though some of these groups remain almost indistinguishable from the Witnesses on doctrinal matters.

So, the Watchtower organization does not stand alone as a separate entity totally unrelated to and apart from what it disdainfully refers to as "the churches of Christendom." Actually, it is very much a part of that grouping of religious bodies that claim to follow Christ, albeit nestled in among other heretical groups at an extreme end of the nominally "Christian" spectrum.

The true Church, however, is not one of "the churches," one of the organizational divisions of Christendom. According to Hebrews 12:23 the true Church is "the congregation of the firstborn who have been enrolled in the heavens" (NWT), "the Church of the first-born whose names are written in Heaven." (Phillips) It is a spiritual entity encompassing all those who belong to Christ.

The tendency to stress membership in an earthly organization manifested itself even among the Apostles, but Jesus set them straight on the matter: "John said to him, 'Teacher, we saw a man who was driving out demons in your name, and we told him to stop, because he doesn't belong to our group.' 'Do not try to stop him,' Jesus told them, 'because no one who performs a miracle in my name will be able soon after to say bad things about me. For whoever is not against us is for us.'" (Mark 9:38–41 TEV)

Neither national boundaries nor human religious structures can confine the true Church. Rather, wherever they are found, inside of a particular church group or outside, "Those who are led by the Spirit of God are sons of God. For you did not receive a spirit that makes you a slave again to fear, but you received the Spirit who makes you sons. And by him we cry, 'Abba, Father.' The Spirit himself testifies with our spirit that we are God's children." (Romans

8:14–16 NIV) Those who have their eyes on Christ and on his true Church do not let different customs or different clothing or different organizational structures sever the bonds of love that unite them with fellow Christians from other traditions.

This can often be strikingly visible at gatherings of former Witnesses who have come into a personal relationship with God through Jesus Christ as outlined in the New Testament. Some of them may now fellowship with charismatic Christians; others may have joined a fundamentalist church; still others may attend a liberal church; and some may meet with fellow believers in private homes. Yet, they are able to share together in worship and in the work of spreading the Gospel. And it is this unity in diversity that identifies those for whom Christianity is some thing greater than a church or organization on the earth.

See also Unity.

Communion

Jehovah's Witnesses celebrate Communion once a year at their annual "Memorial" service, generally held after sundown on what Watchtower leaders calculate from the lunar calendar to be the Jewish Passover date. Their timing and their use of red wine and unleavened bread may derive from the ceremony Jesus instituted on the night he was to be betrayed, but that is where any resemblance stops.

Whereas Jesus said, "Keep doing this in remembrance of me" (Luke 22:19 NWT) and "'Take, eat.' . . . Also . . . 'Drink out of it, all of you'" (Matthew 26:26–27 NWT), the Watchtower Society instructs the vast majority of its followers not to partake but simply to observe.

"Who, then, may properly partake of the Memorial emblems of the bread and the wine? . . . Those of the 'other

sheep' class are not in the new covenant and so do not partake."

—*The Watchtower*, February 15, 1986,
pages 14–15

Today, there are only a few old-timers among Jehovah's
Witnesses who partake of the communion loaf and cup:

There is only a remnant of such spiritual sons now living,
and these are the ones who properly partake of the
emblems. This, then, accounts for the vast majority of Jehovah's Witnesses being observers and not partakers.

—*The Watchtower*, February 15, 1985,
page 17

The annual service was attended by more than 12,200,000
persons in 1994, according to the January 1, 1995
Watchtower magazine, but only 8,617 partook of the bread
and the cup. Watchtower leaders calculate that these are
the only truly heaven-bound born-again believers alive on
earth today—primarily elderly JWs baptized before the
year 1935—and that these are the only persons entitled to
take Communion. Others are welcome only as observers.
However, with 75,000 Jehovah's Witness congregations
worldwide, this means that at most JW meeting places the
bread and the cup are passed up and down the aisles with
no one taking Communion.

Jesus' words quoted above are that "all of you" should
partake, but Jehovah's Witnesses respond that this
means only "you" who are going to heaven, a small elite
group. The average rank-and-file JW looks forward to
everlasting life on earth, not in heaven, and therefore
does not take Communion. To refute this position it is
necessary to see what the Bible says about who is going
to heaven.

See Heaven *and* Born Again *and* Little Flock.

Cross

Until the late 1920s Watchtower publications commonly referred to Christ's death on a cross and featured artwork depicting it that way. (See, for example, the 1927 book *Creation*, page 209 in early editions, 265 in later editions.) However, JW publications since that time show Jesus nailed to a "torture stake" instead—an upright pole without a crossbeam. Strong statements characterize the Watchtower Society's rejection of the cross.

> "No Biblical evidence even intimates that Jesus died on a cross."
>
> *—Awake!*, November 8, 1972, page 28

> "So, the evidence indicates that Jesus did not die on the traditional cross."
>
> *—Awake!*, September 22, 1974, page 28

Anyone who believes Jesus did die on a cross immediately identifies himself or herself as a "pagan false religionist" in the eyes of loyal Jehovah's Witnesses who accept the Society's teaching that He was put to death on an upright stake or pole. JWs see this not as a minor technicality, but rather as a crucial issue.

Interestingly, though, an illustration on page 7 of the 1990 booklet *How Can Blood Save Your Life?* (currently in use by JWs) shows early Christians in the Roman arena nailed to crosses. Likewise, *The Watchtower* of November 15, 1993, quotes Roman historian Tacitus on the persecution of the early Church. The quote on page 9 includes—perhaps inadvertently—his testimony that early Christians "were nailed up to crosses."

While still featuring an illustration of Jesus nailed to such a "torture stake" with one nail through His hands above His head, the August 15, 1987, *Watchtower* magazine also includes an article titled "Where Were His Legs?"

showing two drawings of a man on a cross and discussing the various possibilities of how Jesus may have been nailed up. On page 29, the article makes these cautiously worded qualifying statements:

> "For instance, as we discussed on page 23, Jesus most likely was executed on an upright stake without any crossbeam. No man can know with certainty even how many nails were used in Jesus' case."
>
> ". . . Thomas later said: 'Unless I see in his hands the print of the nails.' (John 20:25) That could have meant a nail through each hand, or the plural 'nails' might have reference to nail prints in "his hands and his feet." (See Luke 24:39) We cannot know precisely where the nails pierced him, though it obviously was in the area of his hands . . ."
>
> "Thus we recognize that depictions of Jesus' death in our publications, such as you see on page 24, are merely reasonable artistic renderings of the scene, not statements of anatomic absolutes. Such depictions need not reflect the changing and conflicting opinions of scholars, and the drawings definitely avoid religious symbols that stem from ancient paganism."

While here admitting uncertainty about the manner of crucifixion, the *Watchtower* continues to attack the cross by pointing out the pagan religious use of crosses before the time of Christ. Distasteful as it may be, however, the Lord was in fact executed by pagan Romans, who would not have hesitated to use one of their pagan crosses as the instrument of execution.

Which instrument of execution fits the biblical accounts of Christ's death? Thomas said, "Except I shall see in his hands the print of the nails . . ." indicating that there was not just a single nail in Jesus' hands as in Watchtower illustrations, but two or more nails such as would be needed to pin his hands to the opposite ends of a crossbeam. (John 20:25 KJV) Matthew also notes, "Above his head they placed the written charge against him . . ." (Matthew 27:37 NIV) If

Christ had been nailed to an upright stake with his hands above his head as in Watchtower illustrations, Matthew would more likely have said that the written charge was placed above his hands; since he actually did say "above his head," this would imply that Jesus' hands were someplace else—at the ends of a crossbeam.

In addition to the above, Scripture indicates that Jesus set out for Calvary "carrying his own cross." (John 19:17 NIV) A man could not carry the massive cross that illustrations sometimes show Christ nailed to. Nor could a man carry the Watchtower's "torture stake"—any more than a man could carry a telephone pole. But a man could, with great difficulty, carry a crosspiece that he would be nailed to and that would then be hoisted by ropes onto an upright piece that was permanently set in the ground. This, according to scriptural and archaeological evidence, is the sort of instrument on which Christ died.

Cult Charges

Are Jehovah's Witnesses a cult? Many voices must be saying so, or why else would six pages—including the cover—of the February 15, 1994 *Watchtower* magazine be devoted to answering this charge? The Watchtower Society's answer comes in the form of two articles: "Cults— What Are They?" (pages 3–4) and "Are Jehovah's Witnesses a Cult?" (pages 5–7).

Above a half-page photo of the burning Waco, Texas, compound of David Koresh and his Branch Davidians the first article begins by summarizing that recent tragedy— strangely without ever naming the town of Waco or mentioning cult leader David Koresh or his sect by name. The article then refers to the 1969 Charles Manson murders, the 1978 Jonestown disaster, and the 1987 mass-suicide of a pseudo-Christian cult in Korea. Next, after noting the existence of organizations set up to monitor cults, and the anticipated proliferation of cults surrounding the advent of the year 2000, *The Watchtower* goes on to ask in a new subheading, "What Is a Cult?"

It turns for the answer to such authorities as *The World Book Encyclopedia*, *Newsweek* magazine, and *Asiaweek* magazine to come up with definitions centering on the thought of "small, fringe groups" which follow "a single, charismatic individual," "a living leader who promotes new and unorthodox doctrines and practices," or "a charismatic leader, who often proclaims himself to be the personification of God." To this it goes on to add from another source the thought of a group "employing unethically manipulative techniques of persuasion and control to advance the goals of its leaders." Then *The Watchtower* comments in its own words that "Usually they conduct their religious activities in secrecy," and, "Many of these cultic groups actually isolate themselves in communes."

Finally, the article states the problem:

> "Occasionally, anticult organizations and the media have referred to Jehovah's Witnesses as a cult. A number of recent newspaper articles lump the Witnesses with religious groups known for their questionable practices."

The second article, titled "Are Jehovah's Witnesses a Cult?" goes on to offer "evidence" that they are not. It is only fair to examine that alleged evidence point by point:

• *Jesus and his disciples were falsely accused*

Yes, they were. But that does not mean that the same is true of Jehovah's Witnesses. The argument that "they persecuted Jesus too" has been used by countless cults, including the Branch Davidians of Waco, Texas. It has nothing to do with the guilt or innocence of the group in question.

The Watchtower's use of such an argument is merely a tricky debating tactic, not a valid response to critics.

> **• a Russian official who had been told Jehovah's Witnesses were an "underground sect sitting in darkness and slaughtering children and killing themselves" discovered them instead to be "normal, smiling people"**

Use of this story, too, is a deceptive trick known as a "straw man" argument. *The Watchtower* sets up a fake "straw man"—the extremely inaccurate description of JWs the official first heard—and then easily knocks down that straw man. Of course, "normal, smiling people" can be found in many cults, including those cited earlier for their mass suicides.

The fact that *The Watchtower*'s first two defenses consist of clever tricks instead of real evidence should make readers even more cautious in examining the remaining arguments:

> **• their meetings consist of Bible study and discussion**

The same was true of the meetings David Koresh conducted with his Branch Davidians at the Waco compound. His lectures revolved around the book of Revelation and other Bible prophecies. Cults and heretical sects have been twisting scripture from the days of the apostles. (2 Peter 3:16)

> **• their activities are public, not secretive**

While it is true that house-to-house preaching is a public activity and most JW meetings are open to the public, there is much about the organization that remains hidden from the public eye. Most outsiders have no idea of the extent to which the Watchtower Society controls its members—punishing them if they vote in elections, hang an evergreen wreath on their door at Christmastime, or read forbidden literature (such as this book you are now reading!). Even most relatives and neighbors are unaware that JWs can be put on trial behind closed doors, without right to representation by an attorney, and that they can be commanded to shun a life-long friend without even being informed of the friend's alleged offense against the organization.

• *with more than 11 million people attending, they are "far from being a small fringe cult"*

True, the numbers involved exclude Jehovah's Witnesses from the category of a small fringe cult, but this does not exclude them from being a large major cult.

• *victims of alleged brainwashing are lacking*

To the contrary there are countless former members who testify to having been brainwashed, plus unbiased secular authorities who confirm their testimony. For example, consider the book *Combatting Cult Mind Control* by Steven Hassan (Park Street Press, 1988). Far from being an anti-Witness publication, it does not discuss JWs at all in the body of the book. Yet, it routinely lists Jehovah's Witnesses among the cultic groups in its appendix.

• *"'They are people who are absorbed in humanity.' And they do not live in communes, isolating themselves from relatives and others."*

Aside from the roughly 15,000 full-time volunteers who live and work at the sect's office/factory/farm facilities, most JWs are not physically isolated. But they are socially isolated from outsiders. And when contact with "worldly" (non-member) relatives or neighbors does take place, Witnesses are taught to view this as an opportunity for witnessing rather than a time for fellowship. The statement quoted here denying that JWs isolate themselves is propaganda for public consumption; on page 24 of this same *Watchtower* issue Witnesses themselves are told, "We must also be on guard against extended association with worldly people. Perhaps it is a neighbor, a school friend, a workmate, or a business associate. . . . What are some of the dangers of such a friendship? . . ."

So, not only do JWs in fact isolate themselves, but their leaders are deliberately concealing this fact and falsifying information to defend themselves against the charge of being a "cult."

• *they adhere strictly to the Bible*

Again, this same claim is made by most pseudo-Christian cults, including the one whose members died in the fire at Waco; surviving children felt left out when the others "went to heaven." The Watchtower organization goes a step further than most cults, actually replacing standard Bibles with those tailored to fit the sect's doctrines, rather than relying simply on unique interpretation.

• *"the veneration and idolization of human leaders so characteristic of cults today is not to be found among Jehovah's Witnesses"*

The Watchtower has acknowledged elsewhere that early Witnesses "were exalting creatures, indulging in a personality cult that focused on Charles T. Russell." (May 1, 1989, page 4) Witnesses today exalt their collective leadership as a group. They view their organization as essential to salvation and feel obligated to obey its every command. They call it "Mother" (God is "Father"), "God's channel of communication," "God's organization," and pledge to it their full loyalty and allegiance. In effect, they idolize the organization as a corporate savior and lord. Thus, while it is true that they are no longer a cult focused on an individual, today's JWs are a cult focused on an organization.

Even worse, Jehovah's Witnesses are a deadly cult. A single sentence in the February 15, 1994 *Watchtower* article admits, without comment, "They will not eat blood, nor will they accept blood transfusions." (page 7) But it fails to mention that this ban on blood transfusions has caused more deaths than the Waco, Texas standoff, the Manson murders, and the Jonestown mass suicide put together. (*See* Blood Transfusions.)

Instructions on page 31 of the June 15, 1991 *Watchtower* tell Witnesses even to "resist a blood transfusion that has been ordered or authorized by a court." They are to "avoid being accessible" for such a court-ordered transfusion by fleeing the scene, or else follow the example of a 12-year-old girl who had been taught to "fight any court-authorized transfusion with all the strength she could muster, that she would scream and struggle, that she would pull the injecting device out of her arm and would attempt to destroy the blood in the bag over her bed." This course is to be followed even if such action might make the Jehovah's Witness "a lawbreaker or make him liable to prosecution" by the authorities. Witnesses have been jailed for carrying out such instructions, even kidnapping children from hospital beds and taking them out hospital windows.

Why is it that the news media and the general public fail to put Watchtower leaders in the same class with David Koresh and Jim Jones? Partly because the deaths of JWs refusing blood products have occurred—and continue to occur—one at a time in different locations, rather than in one spot where TV cameras could focus. And partly because the Watchtower Society continues to use its mammoth propaganda machine to clean up its image. The February 15, 1994 *Watchtower* article asking, "Are Jehovah's Witnesses a Cult?" is a prime example.

Death

According to the chapter "What Happens at Death?" in the book Jehovah's Witnesses use to instruct new converts, death is a "state of nonexistence . . . a state of complete unconsciousness" and "the dead cannot do anything and cannot feel anything. They no longer have any thoughts." (*You Can Live Forever in Paradise on Earth*, 1989 edition, pages 76–77) To prove that "the Bible shows this" to be the actual condition of the dead, the book refers to Ecclesiastes 9:5, 10 ("For the living know that they shall die; *but the dead know not any thing* . . . there is no work . . . nor knowledge, nor wisdom, in the grave, whither thou goest."). Then it turns to Psalm 146:3–4 for proof that when "earthling man" dies, "His spirit goes out, he goes back to his ground; *in that day his thoughts do perish.*" The book italicizes in each passage the key words that seem to indicate a state of unconscious nonexistence for the dead.

Is that what the Bible actually teaches? Or are the JWs pulling verses out of context and misinterpreting them? That the latter is the case with Psalm 146:3–4 can be established simply by reading all ten verses of that Psalm together. It immediately becomes apparent that the Psalmist is not speaking about the condition of the dead, but rather is contrasting the hope enjoyed by those who trust in God with the false hope of those who put their confidence in human leaders. While "the LORD shall reign forever" (verse 10), the human prince dies and with him dies all that he had thought or intended to do. On the day of his death "his plans perish," as the *Revised Standard Version* renders the last words of verse 4; "all his schemes perish" (*Jerusalem Bible*). The verse does not teach that the dead are unconscious, as the Watchtower Society claims. The subject of the afterlife is not even addressed in Psalm 146.

On the other hand, Ecclesiastes 9:5, 10 does say that "the dead know nothing" (RSV), but the entire book of Ecclesiastes is written in a sort of point-counterpoint style expressing in negative terms the skeptic's hopeless despair and then eventually responding to this with positive expressions of faith. To take verses 5 and 10 as the final word on the matter would be akin to reading Luke's account of the temptation in the wilderness and then building doctrine on what the devil said rather than on Christ's response. To help a JW see this to be the case, ask him if he believes that God will reward His faithful servants of Old Testament times in a resurrection of the righteous. The Witness will answer, Yes. Then direct his attention away from the few words the sect's leaders always focus on in Ecclesiastes 9:5 and ask him to look at the rest of the verse and the immediate context. It declares that those who die have *no* reward, no future—a thought obviously at odds with the rest of the Bible. (Compare Revelation 11:18.) Ask the Witness if he truly believes the pronouncement of verse 2 that "one fate comes to all, to the righteous and the wicked, to the good and the evil." (RSV) Perhaps he will begin to see that this portion of Ecclesiastes expresses the skeptic's hopeless despair. Further along, the book of Ecclesiastes concludes by refuting these thoughts with the positive assurance that "man goes to his eternal home . . . the dust returns to the earth as it was, and the spirit returns to God" who "will bring every deed into judgment, with every secret thing, whether good or evil." (Ecclesiastes 12:5, 7, 14 RSV) For more on these verses and other passages Jehovah's Witnesses twist when discussing the condition of the dead, see my book *Jehovah's Witnesses Answered Verse by Verse*.

Elsewhere the Bible abounds with references showing that persons who die continue to exist in a conscious state apart from their bodies. God commanded the Jews not to call up the dead. (Deuteronomy 18:11) Saul violated this command and had Samuel called up:

> "Now Samuel was dead, and all Israel had lamented him, and buried him . . . And Samuel said to Saul, Why hast thou disquieted me, to bring me up? . . . the LORD will also deliver Israel with thee into the hand of the Philistines: and to mor-row shalt thou and thy sons be with me." (1 Samuel 28:3, 15, 19)

God commanded Isaiah to taunt the king of Babylon with words such as these: "The grave below is all astir to meet you at your coming; it rouses the spirits of the departed to greet you . . . they will say to you, 'You also have become weak, as we are; you have become like us.'" (Isaiah 14:9–10 NIV) Jesus said not to fear "them which kill the body, but are not able to kill the soul." (Matthew 10:28) Rather, he said to "Fear him, which after he hath killed hath power to cast into hell." (Luke 12:5) If a person's conscious existence ended at death, these statements by Christ would make no sense.

In his parable of the rich man and Lazarus, Jesus tells us, "the beggar died, and was carried by the angels into Abraham's bosom: the rich man also died, and was buried; And in hell he lifted up his eyes, being in torments." (Luke 16:22–23)

See Heaven, Hell, *and* Paradise. *Also* Soul & Spirit *and* Resurrection.

Deity

Jehovah's Witnesses believe that God the Father is the Almighty God, the God of the Bible. They believe that Jesus Christ is "a god" or "divine" only in the sense that angels can be described in those terms, because they accept the teaching that he was not God incarnate, but Michael the Archangel born in human flesh. Witnesses do not speak of "the Holy Spirit"; instead they refer to "holy spirit," without the definite article and not capitalized, in the belief that these words identify neither God nor any person at all, but rather an impersonal "active force" that God uses to accomplish his will.

It is not surprising, then, that Christians choose this subject more than any other when first entering discussions with Jehovah's Witnesses to Christ. The reason for this appears to be two-fold: first, it is the area in which Jehovah's Witnesses appear most obviously in error, and second, since it is such a basic and elementary part of orthodox doctrine, it is the subject Christians feel most confident and comfortable discussing without any special preparation. However, with few exceptions, this choice of subject matter is an unfortunate one. I could compare it with an eye surgeon who sees a patient with bulging eyes and decides to operate because the problem is obviously in the eyes and because the scalpel is the instrument he is most confident and comfortable using—when the patient's eye problem is actually just a symptom of thyroid imbalance. Just as eye surgery would only make matters worse for such a patient, in the same manner pressing a JW on the subject of deity often serves only to cement the Witness more firmly in the Watchtower organization. My own experience on the receiving end of such efforts illustrates this point.

One day in the late 1970s, when I was a Jehovah's Witness elder, I boldly walked into the fellowship hall of an Assembly of God church in Brockton, Massachusetts, where a counter-cult ministry was operating a literature table. While the other Witnesses who were out in field service with me waited outside in my car, I began witnessing to the bushy-haired young fellow who was manning the table. He responded by questioning me about the Watchtower Society's prediction that 1975 would bring Armageddon. He showed me photocopies documenting the false prophecy.[4] I responded with the then standard defense that the time interval between the creation of Adam and the creation of Eve would allow for some years after 1975. He, in turn, showed me the *Aid to Bible Understanding* article on Eve (page 538) which gave her age as the same as Adam's.[5]

The young Christian's presentation was really beginning to shake me, and I wanted to hear more. If the Watchtower Society was not a true spokesman for God, I wanted to know the facts. Just then, however, the pastor of the church walked up to us and took charge of the discussion, turning it to the subject of the Trinity. I was certain that the Trinity doctrine was false, and I was well-prepared to use Scripture in support of JW theology, but I saw no point in wasting time arguing with a man determined to force on me what I viewed as worship of a satanic three-headed false god. So, I politely excused myself and left.

For some time, whenever I recalled the incident, I wished I could have heard the rest of what the young man had to say about false prophecies in Watchtower literature; but then I would remember the pastor's pushy arguments for the Trinity and be glad I left. If I had been allowed at that time to hear all the evidence proving the Watchtower Society to be a false prophet, perhaps I would not have remained in the organization until 1982.

Like the previously mentioned patient whose thyroid problem manifested itself in bulging eyeballs, my erroneous theology was a *symptom* of my problem, not the root cause. The well-intentioned pastor took aim at my symptoms, but it was the young man at the counter-cult table who knew enough about JWs to go after the real problem, namely, my looking to the Watchtower Society as the final authority in the matter of deity.

Deity

Rather than start out addressing the issue of deity head-on, the steps that need to be taken with JWs in most cases are these:

(1) Use their own literature to prove the Watchtower Society a false prophet. Show how back-and-forth doctrinal changes prove the organization does not speak for God.

(2) Help the JW see that his or her salvation depends, not on an organization, but on Jesus Christ; also, that Christ deserves obedience as our Lord. An organization claiming we must obey its instructions and depend on it for salvation is a counterfeit lord and savior—a false Christ—so the JW needs to stop following the organization and must turn to Jesus Christ as Savior and Lord.

(3) Now that the organization has been taken out of the way as the authoritative interpreter of Scripture, it becomes possible for the JW to read the Bible with enough understanding to correct his or her theology. You can use the appropriate chapters of this book as a guide to that reeducation, perhaps referring also to *Jehovah's Witnesses Answered Verse by Verse* if particular passages pose a problem.

Unfortunately, Christians who lack first-hand personal experience with JW thinking often start out trying to correct the individual's theology first. They assume that, shown the appropriate Bible verses, the Witness will get the point. But these Christians fail to realize the extent to which mind control blocks any interpretation other than that supplied by the Watchtower Society. For example, I have seen JWs read at Revelation 19:1 the words "great crowd in heaven" and say that the great crowd is not in heaven but on earth—the exact opposite of what the verse says—because the Society has told them authoritatively that the great crowd is not in heaven. A similar mental block occurs when Witnesses read verses about the deity of Christ.

Failure to recognize this can result in Christians actually hindering JWs instead of helping them turn to Christ. That is what happened when the pastor mentioned above interrupted the young man who was effectively breaking through the mind control barrier in my own case. Instead of helping to lead me to Christ, this pastor actually aborted the process altogether. Although he knew his Bible, he did not know Jehovah's Witnesses or how to talk to them.

A similar mistake is made when Christians take the position that JWs worship "a false god" or try to discredit their attachment to "Jehovah." I have heard Christians speak of "the god of the Watchtower" as if he were some foreign god that Witnesses must stop worshiping in order to turn to the God of Christianity. This, however, is not actually the case. JWs are not like worshipers of Baal or Zeus who must be introduced for the first time to the true God; rather, they are like Jews who already have some knowledge of the God of the Bible, but who need to correct some erroneous beliefs and come to "know" him personally through the revelation of Jesus Christ.

Moreover, the only thing accomplished by telling JWs that they worship the wrong God is to erect a greater obstacle to their conversion. Even when addressing the pagan men of Athens who really did worship foreign gods, the Apostle Paul demonstrates compassion and puts to good use his knowledge of how these non-believers think. Instead of starting out attacking them as idolaters and worshipers of false gods, Paul establishes common ground by praising them for being "very religious" and then speaks of their "altar with this inscription: TO AN UNKNOWN GOD. Now what you worship as something unknown I am going to proclaim to you." (Acts 17:23 NIV)

We imitate Paul when we express appreciation for a JW's devotion to God and the Bible, and then demonstrate that the Watchtower organization misrepresents both. When we start out attacking a JW's theology we are often simply placing an obstacle in his path—hindering rather than helping him turn to Christ.

See God, Jehovah, Jesus Christ, *and* Holy Spirit.

Education

The matter of higher education is an issue that may be introduced profitably in discussions with a Jehovah's Witness—especially with one who was raised in the organization. Many children raised as Jehovah's Witnesses have grown up to regret being deprived of the opportunity to receive a college education. A discussion driving home the realization that following the sect's teachings leads to lasting harm may be helpful in getting a JW to reevaluate other Watchtower teachings.

The organization's official position has long been that reading Watchtower literature offers a better education than secular schooling: "Often the very best and most beneficial studying you do is that done when you read a new *Watchtower* or *Awake!* or a new book with the joy of getting the new truths and a fresh view." (*The Watchtower,* June 1, 1967, page 338) And therefore, higher education was viewed as not only unnecessary, but actually a satanic snare to be avoided at all cost:

> Many schools now have student counselors who encourage one to pursue higher education after high school, to pursue a career with a future in this system of things. Do not be influenced by them. Do not let them "brainwash" you with the Devil's propaganda to get ahead, to make something of yourself in this world.
>
> —*The Watchtower,* March 15, 1969,
> page 171

In very recent years, however, the Watchtower Society has softened its policy to the point of now allowing higher education in some instances, at the discretion of parents:

> ... the general trend in many lands is that the level of schooling required to earn decent wages is now higher than it was a few years ago. ... So no hard-and-fast rules should be made either for or against extra education. ... If Christian parents responsibly decide to provide their children with further education after high school, that is their prerogative.
>
> —*The Watchtower*, November 1, 1992, pages 18–20

However, as in the case of Witnesses who went blind or died during the years (1967–1980) when the Society prohibited cornea and organ transplants, those who prematurely ended their schooling and now find themselves working long hours sweeping floors or washing dishes will gain little comfort from the latest changes in Watchtower policy on higher education. They cannot regain the lost years and the lost opportunities.

Not only should this call into question the advisability of following other JW teachings, but it should also give a Witness a preview of what it might be like to end up in "outer darkness" where "there shall be weeping and gnashing of teeth." (Matthew 22:13) How sad it will be to discover, too late, that one followed a false prophet organization instead of receiving salvation at the hand of the Son of God!

Faithful and Discreet Slave

Although the "faithful and wise servant" in Jesus' illustration at Matthew 24:45 draws little more than passing interest from most Bible readers, his identity is a vital issue to Jehovah's Witnesses. Proof that this "faithful and discreet slave" (*New World Translation*) is not who the Watchtower Society says he is may be all that is needed to get a JW to quit the organization.

Who, then, does the Society claim the "faithful and discreet slave" of Matthew 24:45 to be? The answer depends on when you ask the question. Watchtower literature originally identified the "faithful and discreet slave" as "that servant (the whole body of Christ)." (*The Watch Tower*, November 1881, page 291 Society's reprints) It was said to be the entire Christian congregation, collectively.

Later, when "the light got brighter" the Society taught for a number of years that Matthew 24 points to a single individual as the "faithful and discreet slave," namely the sect's founder and first president Charles Taze Russell: "*The Watch Tower* unhesitatingly proclaims brother Russell as 'that faithful and wise servant.'" (*The Watch Tower*, March 1, 1917, page 6049 Society's reprints)

Still later, "the light got brighter" again and the earlier rejected teaching was reinstated: "In February 1927 this erroneous thought that Russell himself was the 'faithful and wise servant' was cleared up." (*1975 Yearbook of Jehovah's Witnesses*, page 88) So, the Society today teaches a collective "servant" made up of the body of Christ or the "anointed class"—the remaining 8000-odd spirit-anointed JW old-timers at the nucleus of the Watchtower organization who claim to be among the 144,000 with a heavenly hope.

Why is correctly identifying the "faithful and discreet slave" so crucial to Jehovah's Witnesses? Because they believe it is their relationship to this "slave" that determines whether or not they are actually Christians, whether or not they can understand the Bible, and whether or not they will receive everlasting life:

The fact is, many things are needed to be a real Christian. . . . a Christian has to recognize the authority of "the faithful and discreet slave."

—*The Watchtower*, October 1, 1991, page 20

Thus, we are enlightened by God's answers to present-day problems, answers that reveal where we are in the stream of time and how we can successfully plan for the future. Those answers come to us through the channel of "the faithful and discreet anointed slave" class, which uses the Watchtower Society as its publishing agency.

—*Awake!*, October 8, 1991, page 13

It is unlikely that someone who simply reads the Bible without taking advantage of divinely provided aids could discern the light. That is why Jehovah God has provided "the faithful and discreet slave," foretold at Matthew 24:45–47. Today that "slave" is represented by the Governing Body of Jehovah's Witnesses.

—*The Watchtower*, May 1, 1992, page 31

The speaker concluded: "Let all zealously continue to support the faithful and discreet slave. It is only by doing this that someday very soon all sheeplike ones will be able to hear the happy words. 'Come, you who have been blessed by my Father, inherit the kingdom . . .'"

—*The Watchtower*, January 15, 1993, page 18

Posing as this "slave," the collective leadership enjoys spiritual authority and temporal power similar to that wielded by medieval popes of the Catholic Church, with the JW faithful being told, "It is vital that we . . . respond to the directions of the 'slave' as we would to the voice of God." (*The Watchtower*, June 15, 1957, page 370)

Is it really true that Jesus "assured us" that "he would raise up a 'faithful and discreet slave' that would serve as his channel of communication," as *The Watchtower* asserts? (October 1, 1994, page 8) How can Christians answer the claim that "... today 'the faithful and discreet slave' is associated with Jehovah's Witnesses and represented by the Governing Body of these Witnesses"? (*The Watchtower*, February 1, 1993, page 16) A convincing answer may lead a Jehovah's Witness out of bondage.

The most effective response is to quote back to the JW some of the things that have been "communicated": false prophecies, doctrinal flip-flops, outright deceptions, and so on—as documented in this book and in other references cited here. (Encourage the Witness to verify the quotes by looking them up at the Kingdom Hall library.) Since these falsehoods could not have originated with God, the Watchtower leaders must have been communicating their own ideas or acting as someone else's "channel of communication," not God's.

Once freed from following the Watchtower, must the former JW now look elsewhere to identify a different "faithful and discreet slave" that God is using today? No. Reading Matthew 24:45–47 in its immediate context—verses 37–51—shows Jesus was merely encouraging each one of his followers to be watchful regarding his coming; he was not appointing any "channel of communication" at all. He showed the outcome for two men in the field, one taken and the other left; two women at the mill; a householder who could turn out to be watchful or careless; and a slave who could turn out to be faithful or evil. That evil slave is *not* someone different from the faithful slave. Verse 48 is still speaking of *the same* slave when it goes on, "But if ever that evil slave should ..." So the point of the parable is that Jesus is encouraging each individual follower to be watchful rather than careless and to be faithful and discreet rather than evil.

Interestingly, the Society's book *Our Incoming World Government—God's Kingdom* admits this on pages 158–159:

The King Jesus Christ detests lukewarm service, half-hearted attention. He wants no hypocrites in his kingdom.

This vital point is emphasized by Jesus Christ in the illustrations of the "faithful and discreet slave" and "that evil slave," the illustrations that he gave right after urging his disciples to "prove themselves ready" at all times. (Matthew 24:45–51) There is a grand reward reserved for Christ's disciples who prove themselves to be faithful, discreet and loving slaves of his, uncompromisingly devoted to his handling of the promised world government.

So, the Watchtower Society itself at one point admitted that Jesus gave this parable to encourage each of his followers individually to be a faithful and discreet slave rather than an evil slave. There is no individual or corporate "slave" that must be looked to today as God's channel of communication.

False Prophecies

From the sect's earliest days to the present, Jehovah's Witnesses have been foretelling what would happen on certain dates, only to be proved wrong when the time arrived.

For example, *The Time is at Hand*, second volume in the Watchtower Society's *Millennial Dawn* or *Studies in the Scriptures* series was published in 1889 with this prophecy: ". . . the final end of the kingdoms of this world, and the full establishment of the Kingdom of God, will be accomplished by the end of A. D. 1914." (page 99)

The seventh volume in the same series, released in 1917 as *The Finished Mystery* features this prophecy on the page following the heading "The Churches Cease To Be":

Also, in the year 1918, when God destroys the churches wholesale and the church members by millions, it shall be that any that escape shall come to the works of Pastor Russell to learn the meaning of the downfall of "Christianity."
—pages 484–485

105

Millions Now Living Will Never Die, a paperback published by the Society in 1920 prophesies that "1925 shall mark the resurrection of the faithful worthies of old" (page 97) and that "we may confidently expect that 1925 will mark the return of Abraham, Isaac, Jacob and the faithful prophets of old" (pages 89–90).

Release of the book *"Life Everlasting—in Freedom of the Sons of God"* in the summer of 1966 triggered considerable prophetic speculation regarding the year 1975, as this magazine article later that year notes with approval:

> It did not take the brothers very long to find the chart beginning on page 31, showing that 6,000 years of man's existence end in 1975. Discussion of 1975 overshadowed about everything else. "The new book compels us to realize that Armageddon is, in fact, very close indeed," said a conventioner.
>
> —*The Watchtower,* October 15, 1966,
> pages 628–629

During the next couple of years articles and convention talks continued to focus on 1975 as the likely time for Armageddon, culminating in a major article titled "Why Are You Looking Forward to 1975?" Like other official pronouncements on the subject, it indicates that the date might be off a bit, but not by more than a few weeks or months— certainly not years:

> Are we to assume from this study that the battle of Armageddon will be all over by the autumn of 1975, and the long-looked-for thousand-year reign of Christ will begin by then? Possibly, but we wait to see how closely the seventh thousand-year period of man's existence coincides with the sabbathlike thousand-year reign of Christ. If these two periods run parallel with each other as to the calendar year, it will not be by mere chance or accident but will be according to Jehovah's loving and timely purposes. . . . It

may involve only a difference of weeks or months, not years.

—*The Watchtower,* August 15, 1968,
pages 494, 499

I was an active Witness myself at that time, and I put off having needed dental work done, in the expectation that 1975 or 1976 at the latest would bring Christ's millennial reign and a restoration of perfect health. The Society used its internal *Kingdom Ministry* monthly to encourage even greater steps of faith in the 1975 prophecy:

"Reports are heard of brothers selling their homes and property and planning to finish out the rest of their days in this old system in the pioneer service. Certainly this is a fine way to spend the short time remaining before the wicked world's end."

—*Kingdom Ministry,* May, 1974, page 3

Painfully conscious of the need to defend themselves against the charge of being false prophets due to the failure of Armageddon to occur by 1975, Watchtower leaders have used extra caution since then when making predictions. Nonetheless, they have continued to make such predictions. One technique they have employed is to say enough to convince Jehovah's Witnesses of the likelihood of Armageddon by a certain date, without actually spelling it out in black-and-white. In this way they inspire their followers to put extra time into their door-to-door work in a final home-stretch effort—without leaving an incriminating trail of failed prophetic quotes.

Thus *Watchtower* and *Awake!* articles in October 1985 tied in the United Nations proclamation of 1986 as an "International Year of Peace" with the biblical warning, "Whenever it is that they are saying: 'Peace and security!' then sudden destruction is to be instantly upon them . . ."

(1 Thessalonians 5:3 *New World Translation*). The October 1 and 15 *Watchtower* magazine covers displayed photos of U.N. headquarters, along with the bold headline "PEACE AND SECURITY". Although unrecognizable to outsiders as a prophecy that 1986 would see the end of the world, the message came across loud and clear to JWs and sent them practically running from door to door to sound the final warning.

Less than two years later the April 8, 1988, *Awake!* magazine added to its prophecy of "a peaceful and secure new world before the generation that saw the events of 1914 passes away" (page 4) the authoritative statement that "The Hebrews . . . reckon seventy-five years as one generation . . ." (page 14). Jehovah's Witness readers worldwide added 75 years to 1914, and come up with 1989. Without coming right out and saying that 1989 would bring Armageddon, *Awake!* concluded the discussion of 1914 and the 75-year generation by saying, ". . . today, most of the generation of 1914 has passed away. . . . Jesus' words will come true, 'this generation will certainly not pass away until all these things have happened.' This is yet another reason for believing that Jehovah's thieflike day is imminent." (page 14) Although they avoided making another statement that could be quoted later as a false prophecy, Watchtower leaders still created in JW minds great expectations for the year 1989.

These subtle predictions for 1986 and 1989 are cited here as evidence that the corporate false prophet has not repented. However, the earlier, more blatant predictions for 1914, 1918, 1925, and 1975 are easier to quote in discussions with JWs. Still, many Witnesses will find it difficult to believe that the organization actually published such statements. If you show them photostatic copies reproduced in my book *How to Rescue Your Loved One from the Watchtower* they will suspect that the copies were tampered with. Even copies furnished by the impartial Inter-library Loan network from Watchtower originals in public libraries may be regarded with suspicion. You will do well to suggest to a JW that he or she confirm the quotes by comparing them with originals in Kingdom Hall libraries or in the personal libraries of long-time Jehovah's Witnesses. (The quotes supplied above are but a small sampling of more than a hundred prophetic quotes listed in my *Index of Watchtower Errors* published by Baker Book House in 1990.)

Little comment is needed when presenting this material, since it speaks for itself. The best commentary is that found in Scripture:

> "But a prophet who presumes to speak in my name anything I have not commanded him to say, or a prophet who speaks in the name of other gods, must be put to death." You may say to yourselves, "How can we know when a message has not been spoken by the LORD?" If what a prophet proclaims in the name of the LORD does not take place or come true, that is a message the LORD has not spoken. That prophet has spoken presumptuously. Do not be afraid of him.
> —Deuteronomy 18:20–22 NIV

> And many false prophets shall rise, and shall deceive many.
> —Matthew 24:11 KJV

False Prophets

After furnishing examples of Jehovah's Witnesses' failed prophecies in the previous section, why follow here with another discussing identifying the Witnesses as false prophets? Because the sect's latest defense tactic employs the argument that promoting false prophecies does not make them false prophets.

Until recently JWs were largely unfamiliar with past prophetic failures and would refuse to believe that such prophetic statements had been made. Now, however, with counter-cult groups giving the facts wider publicity, the Watchtower Society has begun teaching JWs to respond that those "mistakes" on dates don't matter, that prophetic failures do not make one a false prophet: ". . . they should not be viewed as false prophets . . . In their human fallibility, they misinterpreted matters." (*Awake!*, March 22, 1993, page 4)

To defeat this argument, a good first step would be to isolate it from the parties involved. Ask the Jehovah's Witness, Would that defense have been valid for a prophet in ancient Israel whose prediction proved false? Deuteronomy 18:20–22 prescribed the death penalty if a prophet's prediction failed, regardless of the reason. Obviously every false prophet in Israel could have said that he "misinterpreted matters" and could have pointed to his own "human fallibility" as the reason his prophecy failed, but Deuteronomy made no provision for such excuses.

Another recent Watchtower defense argues that JW leaders are not false prophets because their failed prophecies were well-intentioned: "Jehovah's Witnesses, in their eagerness for Jesus' second coming, have suggested dates that turned out to be incorrect." (*Awake!*, March 22, 1993, page 4) Does eagerness excuse making false prophecies? Ask the JW to read 1 Samuel 13:8–14 and to comment on whether God accepted Saul's eagerness as a valid excuse for disobedience. God punished Saul in spite of his excuses.

A third Watchtower defense hinges on a technicality: "Never did they say, 'These are the words of Jehovah.'" (*Awake!*, March 22, 1993, page 4) Deuteronomy's condemnation applies if "what a prophet proclaims in the name of the LORD does not take place or come true." (Deuteronomy 18:22 NIV) In whose name has the Watchtower Society prophesied? Ask a JW to open to page 4 of any issue of *Awake!* magazine from March 8, 1988 through October 22, 1995, and have him or her read the last sentence under "Why *Awake!* Is Published." Point out the prophecy that is printed there in each issue to the effect that the end will come "before the generation that saw the events of 1914 passes away."* The sentence introduces this as "the Creator's promise." Similarly, a hundred years ago when the *Watch Tower* set prophetic dates that have since failed, it claimed, "They are, we believe, God's dates, not ours. But bear in mind that the end of 1914 is not the date for the beginning, but for the end of the time of trouble." (July 15, 1894, p. 1677 Society reprints) So, the sect's leaders have indeed made their false prophecies in God's name.

If a Witness objects that Watchtower publications set most of their prophetic dates without declaring the predictions to be "in God's name," call his or her attention to this statement:

> Those who are convinced that *The Watchtower* is publishing the opinion or expression of a man should not waste time in looking at it at all. Those who believe that God uses *The Watchtower* as a means of communicating to his people, or of calling attention to his prophecies, should study *The Watchtower.*
>
> —*The Watchtower*, January 1, 1942,
> page 5

*IMPORTANT NOTE: As this book was going to press, the Watchtower Society began revising end-times prophecies that had outlived their credibility. The October 22, 1995 *Awake!* magazine was the last issue to feature in its masthead the assertion that "the generation that saw the events of 1914" would see this wicked world's end. Articles in the November 1, 1995 *Watchtower* indicated that the Society no longer stood by that prediction. This, in spite of the fact that it had been portrayed as "the Creator's promise." (More than that, *The Watchtower* of May 15, 1984, actually described the prediction as "Jehovah's prophetic word" and added that "Jehovah, who is the source of inspired and unfailing prophecy, will bring about the fulfillment."—pages 6–7) This latest prophetic failure should prove eye-opening to many thinking JWs.

A magazine that claims not to be publishing men's thoughts but rather boasts of being God's means of communicating God's dates cannot later protest that its prophecies were not made in God's name.

In Matthew 7:15–16 Jesus warned specifically, "Watch out for false prophets. They come to you in sheep's clothing, but inwardly they are ferocious wolves. By their fruit you will recognize them. Do people pick grapes from thornbushes, or figs from thistles?" (NIV) People receive false prophecies from false prophets, and that is their recognizable identity—even when they attempt to disguise themselves as harmless sheep.

Flags

Even people who know virtually nothing about Jehovah's Witnesses are usually aware that "they refuse to salute the flag." During World War II many JW children were expelled from public schools for adhering to this policy, and the resulting negative publicity led to mob violence against Witnesses in several communities across the United States. Eventually the U.S. Supreme Court ruled in *Barnette* v. *West Virginia State Board of Education* (1943) that compulsory flag saluting was unconstitutional. The war ended soon after that, and patriotic tempers cooled. In fact, the pendulum has swung so far in the other direction today that JW children standing respectfully with hands at their sides during the classroom ceremony are scarcely noticed amid unruly teens whose acts of disrespect for the flag range from slouching in their seats to mock saluting with raised arm and clenched fist. Flag-burners long ago upstaged non-saluters.

Christians need not feel obligated to persuade JWs that they ought to salute the flag. In fact, it is best to avoid this emotionally charged issue, if possible. Witnesses, like other people in general, respond most readily to gospel preaching that meets them on common ground. Moreover, they can repent, receive Christ, and join a Christian church without ever saluting a flag—so, why place an unnecessary obstacle in their path? The Church includes within its ranks Quakers who will not swear in court and Mennonite conscientious objectors who will not take up arms. Sound biblical wisdom on such matters of conscience can be gained by reading Paul's discussion of vegetarianism in Romans, chapter 14.

The Jehovah's Witnesses' abhorrence of flags, however, goes far beyond mere conscientious refusal to salute. In actual practice, JWs typically avoid flags as much as possible—displaying them neither at home nor at their places of worship. Many Witnesses even avoid using postage stamps featuring pictures of flags. Why such fear of a piece of cloth? Because the Watchtower Society has taught them that flags derive from pagan false worship: "Today state-exalting nations liken their governments to the lion, the bear, the eagle, etc., and place their images upon insignia and standards just as was done from ancient times. Flags were a characteristic feature of Egyptian temples." So says the Watchtower Society's book *Qualified to be Ministers* (1967 revision) on page 272. A flag representing a country is viewed by Jehovah's Witnesses as "an idolatrous symbol" according to the *Awake!* magazine of September 8, 1971, page 12. That article comments that "historical works trace national flags back to the standards used by armies of ancient peoples such as the Egyptians, Persians and Romans."

Strangely, however, the scriptural discussions found in these Watchtower publications fail to make any reference to the way God commanded Israel to use flags:

> And the children of Israel shall pitch their tents, every man by his own camp, and every man by his own standard, according to their hosts. . . . And Jehovah spake unto Moses

and unto Aaron, saying, The children of Israel shall encamp every man by his own standard, with the ensigns of their fathers' houses.

—Numbers 1:52; 2:1, 2 *American Standard Version,*
Watchtower Society's edition

Or, as another version renders it,

The rest of the Israelites shall set up camp, company by company, each man with his own group and under his own banner. . . . The LORD gave Moses and Aaron the following instructions. When the Israelites set up camp, each man will camp under the banner of his division and the flag of his own clan.

—Numbers 1:52; 2:1, 2 *Today's English Version*

The Living Bible paraphrases the same passage this way:

"'Each tribe of Israel shall have a separate camping area with its own flag.' . . . The LORD gave these further instructions to Moses and Aaron: 'Each tribe will have its own tent area, with its flagpole and tribal banner.'"

—Numbers 1:52; 2:1, 2 *The Living Bible*

In earlier years, the Watchtower Society apparently recognized that there was no biblical objection to such use of flags, and those running the organization actually displayed flags at its Brooklyn Bethel headquarters:

Since the Bethel Home was established, in one end of the Drawing Room there has been kept a small bust of Abraham Lincoln with two American flags displayed about the bust. This is deemed entirely proper . . .

—*The Watch Tower,* May 15, 1917,
page 150

Today, however, Jehovah's Witnesses flee from flags with a fear that borders on the superstitious. In their zeal to avoid idolatrously worshiping flags, they have become unbalanced in the opposite direction—a posture that derives not from Scripture, but from the odd interpretations placed on Scripture by their leaders.

God

Jehovah's Witnesses present what is essentially an Old Testament view of God. They assign the Son the position of a created angel, they declare the Holy Spirit to be a mere impersonal force, and they push aside "the name that is above every name" (Philippians 2:9 NIV) to focus instead on the Hebrew tetragrammaton (YHWH = *Jehovah*). When they do acknowledge that Christ is divine, they do so only in the sense that angels are godlike ones, or in the same sense that the devil is "the god of this world." (2 Corinthians 4:4 KJV) Where John 1:1 says "the Word was God," their *New World Translation* renders it to say "the Word was a god." It changes the Holy Spirit to "holy spirit" and changes Genesis 1:2 to say that God's "active force" was used in creation. (*See* New World Translation.)

In place of the Father, the Son, and the Holy Spirit—the triune God revealed in the New Testament—Jehovah's Witnesses are left with a big God, a little god, and a force. Still, enough evidence remains in their own Bible translation to testify abundantly to the full deity of Christ and to the personality and deity of the Holy Spirit. You may wish to encourage a JW to compare the following verses in his or her copy of the *New World Translation*. (Emphasis is added to key words to aid in comparison.) A powerful lesson can be learned from Scripture alone:

"These are the things that he says, '**the First and the Last**,' who **became dead** and came to life [again] . . ."
—Revelation 2:8 NWT

"Look! He **is coming** with the clouds, and every eye will see him, and those who **pierced him**; and all the tribes of the earth will beat themselves in grief because of him. Yes, Amen. 'I am **the Alpha and the Omega**,' says **Jehovah God**, '**the One** who is and who was and **who is coming, the Almighty.**'"

—Revelation 1:7–8 NWT

"Look! **I am coming quickly** . . . I am **the Alpha and the Omega, the first and the last** . . ."

—Revelation 22:12, 13 NWT

"Yes; **I am coming quickly. Amen! Come, Lord Jesus.**"

—Revelation 22:20 NWT

". . . **I am the same One.** I am **the first**. Moreover, I am **the last**. Moreover, my own hand laid the foundation of the earth, and my own right hand extended out the heavens."

—Isaiah 48:12–13 NWT

"And he laid his right hand upon me and said: 'Do not be fearful. I am **the First and the Last**, and the living one; and I **became dead**, but look! I am living forever and ever . . .'"

—Revelation 1:17–18 NWT

". . . and that you may understand that **I am the same One. Before me there was no God formed**, and **after me** there continued to be none. I—I am Jehovah, and **besides me there is no savior.**"

—Isaiah 43:10–11 NWT

(". . . and the Word was **a god**")

—John 1:1 NWT [Watchtower Society's rendering]

"This is what Jehovah has said, . . . 'I am **the first and I am the last**, and besides me there is no God. . . . **Does there exist *a God* besides me? No**, there is no Rock. I have recognized none.'"

—Isaiah 44:6, 8 NWT

Thus the JW *New World Translation* itself inadvertently bears witness that Jesus is not "a god" beside the Almighty God Jehovah. It testifies that Jesus and Jehovah are both "the One" who is coming, "the same One." There are not two *first*'s and two *last*'s, there are not two *alpha*'s and two *omega*'s (the first and last letters of the Greek alphabet), and yet Jesus and Jehovah are both the First and the Last, and they are both the Alpha and the Omega. They are the same One. Scripture says, ". . . and the Word was God" at John 1:1 in numerous translations the Watchtower Society has not tampered with.

How is that possible? Again, Scripture explains:

> "The Son is the radiance of God's glory and the exact representation of his being."—Hebrews 1:3 NIV

> "For in Christ all the fullness of the Deity lives in bodily form . . ."—Colossians 2:9 NIV

See Jesus Christ *and* Holy Spirit.

"God's Organization"

The belief that the Watchtower Bible and Tract Society is "God's organization" on earth is the central and most important doctrine of Jehovah's Witnesses. Followers accept all the sect's other doctrines, not on account of the biblical arguments advanced, but ultimately because the organization decrees these teachings to be true. Other JW beliefs are subject to change as the organization reveals "new truths" from God.

Where did this organization come from, and how did it acquire such authority? Most Jehovah's Witnesses feel that they are familiar with the sect's history. In their own publications, its origin is usually presented this way:

"God's Organization"

> In the early 1870's a group of ernest, open-minded Bible students started to meet for an unbiased study of God's Word.
>
> —*The Watchtower,* December 1, 1981, page 21

No indication is given here that would indicate that the sect began as a splinter-group breaking away from another existing church. Yet, the facts recorded in older Watchtower literature and outside sources reveal that the group actually did begin as a break-off from the Second Adventists. A young Adventist named Charles Taze Russell, who was serving as assistant editor for an Adventist magazine, left that group, taking others with him, and began publishing a rival magazine which he called *Zion's Watch Tower and Herald of Christ's Presence.* (*See* Adventist Origins.) Current Watchtower literature obscures this fact, apparently because Jehovah's Witnesses today are strongly warned against following "a breakaway group, thus forming a sect . . ." (*Revelation, Its Grand Climax At Hand!,* 1988, page 45) It would be rather incongruous to admit that their own founder began as an "apostate" breaking away from another church.

From such small beginnings the sect has grown phenomenally. The January 1, 1995 Watchtower reports more than 12,200,000 now attend meetings worldwide. Jehovah's Witnesses are the second largest religion in Poland, Italy, Spain, and Portugal, according to an official at Watchtower headquarters who chose to remain anonymous when we interviewed him over the phone. Besides nearly 2 million in the United States, Jehovah's Witnesses also boast of more than a million people attending their meetings in Brazil and another million in Mexico, with figures for meeting attendance falling in the 1/4- to 1/2-million range for Colombia, Germany, Italy, Japan, Nigeria, Philippines, Zaire, and Zambia. Attendance approaches the 1/4-million mark in Argentina, Britain, France, Poland, and Venezuela.

The Watchtower headquarters complex in the Brooklyn Heights section of New York City consists of more than thirty buildings with a current real estate value of $186 million, according to *The New York Times* (November 29, 1992, page 46). Watchtower Farms and other land holdings in Ulster County total nearly $81 million, according to the Middletown, New York *Sunday Record* (October 7, 1990, pages 8 and 31). The organization is also in the process of constructing a $125 million Watchtower Educational Center—comparable to an entire college—on a 700-acre parcel of land near Patterson, New York. Moreover, the sect owns mammoth branch offices and printing factory complexes in dozens of foreign countries, numerous large assembly halls, and the Kingdom Halls where many of its 75,000 local congregations meet. Who could avoid being impressed?

The Witnesses themselves, however, go beyond merely being impressed. Their devotion to the organization approaches idolatrous proportions. In large, bold print on its front cover *The Watchtower* of March 1, 1979, urges readers to "PUT FAITH in a VICTORIOUS ORGANIZATION." And Watchtower leaders today continue to present their organization as an object of faith for their followers; they urge people to "come to Jehovah's organization for salvation." (*The Watchtower*, November 15, 1981, page 21) Obedience to the organization must be unquestioning: "Avoid independent thinking . . . questioning the counsel that is provided by God's visible organization." (*The Watchtower*, January 15, 1983, page 22) They are told that their lives depend on it: "Jehovah is using only one organization today to accomplish his will. To receive everlasting life in the earthly Paradise we must identify that organization and serve God as part of it." (*The Watchtower*, February 15, 1983, page 12)

Since they must come to it for salvation, the organization becomes, in effect, the savior for Jehovah's Witnesses. And, since they must give it unquestioning obedience, the organization becomes their lord. This borders on idolatry. In fact, the Watchtower Society has acknowledged in the past that an organization can actually become an object of idolatrous worship:

> If one renders obedient service to someone or some organization, whether willingly or under compulsion, looking up to such as possessing a position of superior rulership and great authority, then that one can Scripturally be said to be a worshiper.
> —*The Watchtower,* September 1, 1961, page 525

In connection with *other* groups it warns people against becoming "idolatrous worshipers of a man-made organization." (*The Watchtower,* December 1, 1971, page 723) Yet, this sin of idolatry that they are quick to point out in others, Jehovah's Witnesses cannot see in themselves.

The Watchtower's founder and first president, Charles Taze Russell, however, saw the danger of putting faith in an organization, and he warned against it in early issues of the same magazine that now promotes it:

> There is no *organization* today clothed with such divine authority to imperiously command mankind. There is no *organization* doing this today; though we are well aware that many of them claim in theory that they *ought* to be permitted to do so; and many more would like to do so.
> This was the fatal mistake into which the church began to fall in the second century; and the effort to realize this false conception culminated in the boastful, imperious counterfeit of the *coming* kingdom in the Papacy . . .
> —*Zion's Watch Tower,* September, 1893, pages 266–267

Beware of "organization." It is wholly unnecessary. The Bible rules will be the only rules you will need. Do not seek to bind others' consciences, and do not permit others to bind yours. Believe and obey so far as you can understand God's Word . . .

—*Zion's Watch Tower,* September 15, 1895, page 216

Today's Watchtower organization now ignores these instructions of its founder, and instead practices the very things that Russell condemned.

Even more serious is the departure from the biblical pattern of the early Church. Christ Jesus did not set up his apostles as a visible organization so that future disciples could put faith in *them.* Rather, he referred to future disciples as "those putting faith in *me* through their word." (John 17:20 NWT) The apostles taught new disciples to put faith in Jesus Christ, not in themselves. When the men of Lystra attempted to offer sacrifices to Paul and Barnabas, "they ripped their outer garments and leaped out into the crowd, crying out and saying: 'Men, why are you doing these things? We also are humans having the same infirmities as you do . . .'" (Acts 14:14–15 NWT) Similarly, when preaching to the men of Corinth, Paul minimized his own role, so that their "faith might be, not in men's wisdom, but in God's power." (1 Corinthians 2:5 NWT) Rather than put faith in a man-made organization, the Bible's encouragement is to "put your faith in the name of the Son of God." (1 John 5:13 NWT)

To prove that the Watchtower Society is not God's organization, one need only examine its man-made beginnings (*See* Adventist Origins.), its doctrinal flip-flops (*See* New Light.), and its failed prophecies. (*See* False Prophecies *and* False Prophets.)

Gospel

If you ask Jehovah's Witnesses why they are knocking at your door, this is the Bible verse they are most likely to read aloud in response: "And this good news of the kingdom will be preached in all the inhabited earth for a witness to all the nations; and then the end will come." (Matthew 24:14 NWT) "We came to your door to share the gospel with you," they may add, "the good news of God's kingdom."

When Jehovah's Witnesses read that same verse among themselves, however, they often read it differently with extra emphasis on the word *this.* Among themselves they discuss the fact that "*this* good news of the kingdom" or "*this* gospel of the kingdom" is different from the gospel preached by the apostles and by Christian missionaries for nearly 1900 years.

They believe that Jesus Christ returned invisibly in the year 1914 A.D. and "established" God's kingdom in heaven at that time, with the Watchtower Society as his visible agency on earth. The good news or gospel they preach is *this* gospel—the good news that Christ has already returned invisibly.

Witnesses will freely acknowledge that "*this* good news" which they preach is not the same as the Gospel or Good News preached by Christians down through the centuries. They see nothing wrong with this; in fact, they think it is wonderful that they have a different good news:

> ". . . the Kingdom witnessing of Jehovah's Witnesses since 1914 has been something far different from what Christendom's missionaries have published both before and since 1914. 'Different'—how so? . . . What Jehovah's Witnesses have preached world wide since 1918 is something unique . . . the preaching of this good news of the Messianic kingdom as having been established in the heavens in 1914 . . ."
>
> —*The Watchtower,* October 1, 1980,
> pages 28–29

The Bible, on the other hand, plainly warns *against* the preaching of a different gospel. Even the JW *New World Translation* contains this warning:

However, even if we or an angel out of heaven were to declare to you as good news something beyond what we declared to you as good news, let him be accursed. As we have said above, I also now say again, Whoever it is that is declaring to you as good news something beyond what you accepted, let him be accursed.

—Galatians 1:8–9

Ask the Jehovah's Witness, "Did the Apostle Paul teach the disciples in Galatia that Christ would return in 1914 and set up a visible organization with headquarters in Brooklyn, New York?" If not, then the Watchtower's "good news" is "something beyond what the Galatians accepted"—placing Jehovah's Witnesses under God's curse for teaching another gospel.

Governing Body

The worldwide organization of Jehovah's Witnesses is ruled today by a secretive Governing Body of some twelve men (the number varies with deaths and new appointments) based in Brooklyn, New York. The textbook used to introduce potential new converts to the organization likens the members of the Governing Body to Christ's twelve apostles:

The men of that governing body, like the apostles and older men in Jerusalem, have many years of experience in God's service . . . they follow the example of the early governing body in Jerusalem . . .

—*You Can Live Forever in Paradise on Earth*, page 195

In actual practice Jehovah's Witnesses view Governing Body members as possessing apostolic authority and prestige. This is a contradiction, however, because the Society has stated elsewhere (in the context of attacking the Catholic Church) that the "doctrine that the 12 apostles have successors to whom authority has been passed by divine appointment" is *"Not a Bible teaching."* (*Reasoning from the Scriptures,* page 37)

Until the 1970s the Governing Body was considered to be synonymous with the seven-member Board of Directors of the Watch Tower Bible and Tract Society of Pennsylvania. The Board acted as a rubber stamp for the Society's founder and first president Charles Taze Russell. His successor "Judge" Rutherford soundly defeated a hostile Board and thereafter exercised one-man rule. Third president Nathan Knorr weakened as he aged until, early in the 1970s vice-president Frederick Franz introduced "new light" that gave the Governing Body a life of its own. It was expanded to its present size and was elevated to a position above the various legal corporations the sect uses to own property and transact business.

These legal entities—the Watch Tower Bible and Tract Society of Pennsylvania, the Watchtower Bible and Tract Society of New York, Inc., the International Bible Students Association in Great Britain, and so on—are corporations with interlocking boards of directors and are bound to some extent by laws regulating nonprofit corporations. The Governing Body, however, now sits outside of and above the entire legally incorporated structure—in position to command the corporate CEOs, yet aloof from the prying eyes of government regulators and sect members alike. Still, collective leadership helps to prevent the sort of luxurious excesses with which "Judge" Rutherford indulged himself. Today's Governing Body members seem content with power and prestige, together with a relatively spartan lifestyle.

It is at the secret meetings of the Governing Body that doctrine is formulated with "new truths" replacing "old light" upon a two-thirds majority vote. The top-level goings-on behind these closed doors came into public view for the first time in 1983 when former Governing Body member Raymond Franz published his book *Crisis of Conscience.* Jehovah's Witnesses read this exposé at the risk of being disfellowshiped for possessing apostate literature, but those who do examine its evidence often quit the sect voluntarily before a judicial committee can take action against them. Because it meets them on common ground, *Crisis of Conscience* is usually the most effective book to give to a JW beginning to question his or her beliefs.

See also Faithful and Discreet Slave.

Grace

If you tell a Jehovah's Witness that you want to discuss grace, he or she may well respond, "Grace who?" It seems that the average JW is more familiar with Grace as a feminine first name than as a biblical concept.

In part, this is due to the fact that their *New World Translation* renders the Greek word CHARIS (χάρις) as "undeserved kindness" rather than as "grace." This, in itself, is not a problem. "Undeserved kindness," is indeed a valid translation, similar to *The Twentieth Century New Testament's* rendering "loving-kindness" and Charles B. Williams' rendering "unmerited favor." The real problem is that Jehovah's Witnesses fail to grasp that salvation is truly "undeserved" and "unmerited." Generations of Christians have received assurance from the precious words of Ephesians 2:8, "For by grace are ye saved through faith; and that not of yourselves: it is the gift of God," but Jehovah's Witnesses tend to pass over that verse. They miss "the grace of God that bringeth salvation" (Titus 2:11) apart from works.

Their organization is responsible for this, because it teaches them that salvation hinges on affiliation with the Watchtower Society and obedient participation in its works program. (*See* Salvation.) This is nothing new, of course. It is very similar to the false teaching spread abroad in the first century by the Judaizers Paul battled against, and it is similar to the works mentality of the sixteenth century Roman Catholic Church that Martin Luther and other reformers refuted with the Word of God.

No essay need be written here to prove the power of God's grace. The apostle Paul's letter to the Romans already accomplishes that and is the perfect refutation of works-based salvation. Unfortunately, JWs are accustomed to reading Romans—and the rest of the Bible—with Watchtower literature in hand to ensure that only the organization's interpretation is gained from the reading. When I quit the sect and read the epistle itself without a superimposed interpretation, I was overwhelmed.

Can God's free gift be earned by performing works? Paul explains that it would then no longer be a gift: "Now to him that worketh is the reward not reckoned of grace, but of debt." (Romans 4:4) One might expect this to be clear to JWs, since their Bible version speaks of grace as "*unde*-served kindness." "*Un*deserved" means *not* deserved. Yet, in an amazing contradiction not only of Scripture but of the plain meaning of words themselves, an official Watchtower publication speaks of God's undeserved kindness going to those who *deserve* it:

> "We want to give deserving ones the opportunity to learn of Jehovah's undeserved kindness and the Kingdom hope."
>
> —*Our Kingdom Ministry,* December 1993, page 7

Great Crowd

If you ask several different Jehovah's Witnesses why they do not take Communion, why they have no hope of going to heaven, why they feel they are excluded from the body of Christ, all are likely to give the same answer: "I'm a member of the 'great crowd,' not of the anointed class."

Their reference is to the words of Revelation 7:9, as it reads in the JW *New World Translation*:

> After these things I saw, and, look! a great crowd, which no man was able to number, out of all nations and tribes and peoples and tongues, standing before the throne and before the Lamb, dressed in white robes; and there were palm branches in their hands.

They believe this "great crowd" to be a secondary class of believers apart from the body of Christ, and they interpret Revelation 7:9 as a prophecy that such a class would be gathered during the final decades preceding the end of the world.

This teaching originated on May 31, 1935, when Watchtower Society president Joseph F. Rutherford addressed the delegates at a JW convention in Washington, D.C. "There, for the first time, the great multitude (or, great crowd) of Revelation 7:9 was clearly identified in harmony with the rest of the Bible and in accord with events that had already begun to unfold." (*The Watchtower*, February 1, 1995, page 14)

Why did "Judge" Rutherford come up with a new interpretation of this verse that would place new converts from that time onward outside the Christian congregation? Evidently, because the body of Christ was nearly filled to capacity, as he saw it. Jehovah's Witnesses nowadays cite new light from God as the reason for Rutherford's innovation, but a more down-to-earth explanation involves the rapid growth of the JW organization during the 1930s. Long-standing Watchtower doctrine limited the body of Christ to 144,000 individuals, through the sect's interpretation of Revelation 7:4 and 14:1–3, and first century believers had to account for a sizeable portion of that number. Rutherford no doubt noticed that attendance at the annual Memorial service a few weeks before his talk had reached 63,146.

(*Jehovah's Witnesses—Proclaimers of God's Kingdom*, page 717) Simple mathematics revealed that it would soon become necessary to reinterpret the 144,000 as a figurative number or to teach new believers to number themselves among a different group. Rutherford chose the latter course.

From the standpoint of numbers, the Watchtower Society's president made a wise move: with the "great crowd" available to absorb organizational growth, attendance passed the 144,000 mark in the early 1940s and the million mark in the later 1950s. Biblically, however, the doctrine is indefensible. It is accepted only by those who view pronouncements emanating from Watchtower headquarters as if they came from God.

For suggestions on how to refute the JW teaching on the great crowd, see Born Again, Heaven, *and* Paradise.

Heaven

Jehovah's Witnesses believe that, in the year 1935, God stopped calling people to become part of the Christian congregation, the bride of Christ who would eventually go to heaven to live with Christ there. They believe that in that year God began gathering instead a secondary class of believers, outside the body of Christ, whose hope would be to live forever on earth in the flesh. Of the roughly 13 million people attending JW Kingdom Halls worldwide, fewer than 9000 profess to be members of the body of Christ with a heavenly hope. Nearly all of these are elderly folk who joined the sect prior to 1935. The remaining millions see themselves as part of a "great crowd" of believers with an eternal destiny on earth.

The organization teaches new converts that much of what they read in the New Testament does not apply to them, in view of this change God supposedly implemented in 1935. New believers cannot become members of the body of Christ (1 Corinthians 12:27), cannot be "born again" (John 3:3), cannot share in Christ's heavenly kingdom (2 Timothy 4:18), cannot receive the baptism of the Holy Spirit (1 Corinthians 12:13), are not entitled to share in the loaf and cup of communion (1 Corinthians 10:16–17), and so on. In effect, the "1935" doctrine gives Jehovah's Witnesses a relationship with God that is totally different from what is presented in the New Testament.

The sect's leadership—primarily old men who joined under the pre–1935 arrangement—use biblical language to identify themselves as the small "remnant" or few remaining ones of the Spirit-anointed "little flock," Christ's congregation. They promote the thought that their unique status qualifies them to dispense instruction and salvation to the "great crowd" of less privileged "other sheep" who are outside Christ's "little flock." *The Watchtower* explains it this way:

> the spiritual remnant are not envious so as to hold back anything profitable from those "other sheep" but have lovingly published worldwide that grand earthly hope, particularly since the year 1935 . . .
>
> Down to the spring of 1935 the dedicated, baptized witnesses of Jehovah had entertained in true faith the "one hope" that was set before them in Ephesians 4:4–6, as follows: "One body there is, and one spirit, even as you were called in the one hope to which you were called; one Lord, one faith, one baptism; one God and Father of all persons." But in that memorable year of 1935 . . .
>
> —*The Watchtower*, December 15, 1982, page 19

The Watchtower essentially admits that, since 1935, it has directed people away from the one hope, one body, one Lord, one faith, and one baptism outlined for Christians in the New Testament.

129

> ". . . the sheep would inherit the earthly realm . . . Beginning in 1935, 'the faithful slave' has concentrated on locating such sheeplike ones and bringing them into Jehovah's organization."
>
> —*The Watchtower*, February 15, 1995,
> page 8

Where is this teaching found in the Bible, that the call to become part of the body of Christ would end in the year 1935? Nowhere! Witnesses do not even attempt to derive the date from Scripture. Rather, Watchtower leaders say that "light flashed up"—that the organization's president Joseph F. Rutherford received a special "revelation of divine truth"—to introduce this change in 1935:

> These flashes of prophetic light prepared the ground for the historic discourse on "The Great Multitude," given May 31, 1935, by the president of the Watch Tower Society, J. F. Rutherford, at the Washington, D.C., convention of Jehovah's Witnesses. What a revelation of divine truth that was!
>
> —*The Watchtower*, March 1, 1985, page 14

> . . . the heavenly hope was held out, highlighted and stressed until about the year 1935. Then as "light flashed up" to reveal clearly the identity of the "great crowd" of Revelation 7:9, the emphasis began to be placed on the earthly hope.
>
> —*The Watchtower*, February 1, 1982,
> page 28

Outside observers are more likely to conclude that if any "light flashed up" for Joseph Rutherford it was simply a bright idea that occurred to him—not revelation from God, but an idea that Rutherford thought up on his own. Bible readers are forced to this conclusion because the Scriptures discuss in detail the old covenant for the Jews and the new covenant for Christians but make no reference whatsoever to a third arrangement for gathering a "great crowd" after the year 1935.

What does the Bible actually say about the "great crowd" of Revelation 7:9? Is it a secondary class of believers with an earthly hope? Context locates the "great crowd" not on earth, but in the heavenly presence of God. Note the words I have italicized here:

> After these things I saw, and, look! a *great crowd,* which no man was able to number, out of all nations and tribes and peoples and tongues, *standing before the throne and before the Lamb* . . . And they keep on crying with a loud voice, saying: "Salvation [we owe] to our *God, who is seated on the throne,* and to the Lamb." And all the *angels were standing around the throne . . .*
>
> —Revelation 7:9 11 NWT

The Witnesses' own Bible shows the "great crowd" to be standing before God's throne in heaven in company with angels. It is not an earthly scene.

Not only do Jehovah's Witnesses lack biblical support for their claims concerning the "great crowd" and the year 1935, but, in very positive terms, the Bible unmistakably points Christians to their future home in heaven:

> Blessed be the God and Father of our Lord Jesus Christ, which according to his abundant mercy hath begotten us again unto a lively hope by the resurrection of Jesus Christ from the dead, To an inheritance incorruptible, and undefiled, and that fadeth not away, reserved in heaven for you.
>
> —1 Peter 1:3–4

Was this promise of heaven meant only for the apostles and a small number of associates, with new believers after 1935 or some other date excluded from heaven? Not at all. In fact, Jesus prayed to the Father about his apostles, and also about everyone in the future who would believe in him through their word—that they should all end up with him in heaven. He said:

> I make request, not concerning these only, but also concerning those putting faith in me through their word . . . Father, as to what you have given me, I wish that, where I am, they also may be with me, in order to behold my glory.
> —John 17:20, 24 NWT

Have you read the apostles' words, as recorded in the Bible, and put faith in Christ through their word? Then Jesus' prayer applies to you. He wants you to end up with him, where he is, to behold his glory—regardless of whether you came to believe in him before or after 1935.

Why do Watchtower leaders promote a teaching that cuts their followers off from what the New Testament offers to all believers? Power may have something to do with it. As JWs see it, these Watchtower leaders will soon be in heaven ruling as kings over the earth, so it is only proper for the millions who belong to the earthly "great crowd" to submit to their authority, even now. Whatever their motive may be, however, it is a serious matter for Watchtower leaders to imitate the Jewish religious leaders to whom Jesus said,

> Woe to you, scribes and Pharisees, hypocrites! because you shut up the kingdom of the heavens before men; for you yourselves do not go in, neither do you permit those on their way in to go in.
> —Matthew 23:13 NWT

Like the scribes and Pharisees, Watchtower leaders have "shut up the kingdom of the heavens before men"—the millions of men and women they have taught to reject union with Christ and the hope of being with Christ in heaven.

See also Born Again, Great Crowd, *and* Paradise.

Hell

There can be no punishment after death in the Jehovah's Witness scheme of things because the dead cease to exist. They are gone, vanished without a trace. There is no soul or spirit remaining to experience punishment. If that were true, however, what sense would there be to this warning spoken by Jesus Christ?

> "And I say unto you my friends, Be not afraid of them that kill the body, and after that have no more that they can do. But I will forewarn you whom ye shall fear. Fear him, which after he hath killed hath power to cast into hell; yea, I say unto you, Fear him." (Luke 12:4–5)

If the Witnesses were correct, someone whose body had been killed would no longer exist, hence would have nothing to fear from men or from God. Once you pass out of existence, there is no longer anything that *anyone* can do to you. You simply do not exist. However, Jesus warned that there is indeed more that God can do to a person *after* the person has been killed.

What? God can cast the person into hell (*Gehenna* in Greek), Jesus said.

The Watchtower Society has assured its followers that this does not involve anything unpleasant happening to a person after death; instead, it represents "complete and everlasting destruction" or "death from which there is no resurrection." (*You Can Live Forever in Paradise on Earth,* page 87) If this were so, however, what reason would there be for someone to *fear* being thrown there after being killed—after already ceasing to exist, in the JW interpretation? Pointing out that Jews who rejected the law of Moses "died without mercy," the writer of Hebrews added, "How much more severely do you think a man deserves to be punished who has trampled the Son of God under foot . . . ? . . . It is a dreadful thing to fall into the hands of the living God." (Hebrews 10:28–31 NIV) Does mere nonexistence fit this description?

Luke does not leave us wondering what Jesus meant when telling us to fear God more than we fear men "that kill the body, and after that have no more that they can do." (Luke 12:4) Chapter 16 of Luke's gospel includes Jesus' story of the rich man and Lazarus. After the rich man "died and was buried" it came about that he was "in torment" crying for pity "because I am in agony in this fire" in "this place of torment." (verses 22–24, 28)

The Watchtower Society tries to dismiss the account of the rich man and Lazarus as a fanciful illustration that says nothing at all about the afterlife. They declare each element of the story to be completely symbolic: Abraham represents God, the rich man represents the Jewish religious leaders, Lazarus represents followers of Jesus, and their deaths represent the changes that took place when God removed his favor from the former and bestowed it on the latter. The Jewish leaders "suffered torments when Christ's followers exposed their evil works." (*You Can Live Forever in Paradise on Earth*, page 89)

However, even if this parable were meant to convey such symbolic meaning, what about the story itself? Jesus' other parables all use true-to-life circumstances to illustrate a point or to teach a lesson. People really did dig in fields and hide buried treasure, prodigal sons really did leave home and squander their money, employers really did hire men to work in vineyards, and so on. If the same pattern holds true, then regardless of any symbolic meaning that might also be attached to it, the story of the rich man and Lazarus would also be based on realistic events: some people such as Abraham and Lazarus are rewarded in the afterlife, while others such as the rich man find themselves in a place of torment.

Unfortunately, just as Jehovah's Witnesses deny what the Bible says about punishment after death, there are other religious people who go overboard in the opposite direction, allowing their imagination to run wild with sadistic glee as they picture devils with pitchforks having a grand time inflicting every brutal torture imaginable on helpless men, women, and children. This approach is every bit as unscriptural as the course JWs take. Revelation 20:10 makes it plain that the devil himself is among those undergoing punishment—not ruling over an evil empire in hell. Moreover, the specifics of who else gets thrown into Gehenna and what happens to them there should be imagined—if we must dwell on the subject at all—in the light of all that we know about God's goodness, rather than in the light of Dante's Inferno, Renaissance paintings, or modern works of fiction.

A favorite Jehovah's Witnesses tactic is to draw on the more sadistic popular images of hell, ask you to picture children trapped there and subjected to endless excruciating pain, and then ask, "How could God do such a thing?" However, if Jesus says that wicked men are put outside in the dark to weep and gnash their teeth, we have no business turning this into a picture of children undergoing fiendish torture. If our sensibilities are offended by our concept of hell and who goes there, then perhaps our concept is wrong. God is the one who gave us our sensibilities, our compassion, our fellow-feeling, our inclination to be merciful. He excels over us in all these qualities. The Bible makes it clear that wickedness will be punished after death, righteousness will be rewarded, and Christians have the assurance of eternal life with Christ. But details beyond this are either lacking altogether or are expressed in symbolic language subject to interpretation. Jesus had more to say about hell than anyone else in the Bible, but he is also revealed as far more compassionate and tenderly affectionate than any of us could claim to be. The important thing to remember is that the Judge of all the earth will indeed do what is right, what is fair, and what is good.

(compare Genesis 18:23–33) The solution is not to explain away Scripture to the point of denying its plain meaning, but rather to trust God like little children.

See Heaven, Resurrection, *and* Soul & Spirit

Higher Powers

The identity of "the higher powers" of Romans 13:1–7 is a matter on which the Watchtower Society has done a back-and-forth doctrinal flip-flop and has then attempted to cover up the evidence. It is an excellent subject to bring up in order to document the Jehovah's Witness leadership's unreliability and dishonesty.

The organization started out agreeing with most other commentators that "the higher powers" are human rulers, man's secular governments. Then, a decade after World War I, it switched to saying that "the higher powers" are God the Father and Jesus Christ. The previous view was strongly condemned as among the "false doctrines and practices" that had to be "cleaned out of the organization" according to the Society's 1959 book *Jehovah's Witnesses in the Divine Purpose* (page 91). Finally, though, in 1962 the organization readopted the rejected viewpoint and began teaching, once again, that "the higher powers" are the secular governments. In an attempt to cover up this flip-flop the leaders have presented this as new enlightenment rather than as a return to a previously rejected belief.

Ask the Jehovah's Witness you are speaking with to open his or her copy of *Jehovah's Witnesses—Proclaimers of God's Kingdom,* a colorful volume published by the Watchtower Society in 1993 to teach followers about the sect's history. Have the JW open to pages 146–147 under the heading, "The Light Shines More and More." The book here offers the "progressive understanding" excuse which the Watchtower Society uses to explain its many doctrinal shifts. (*See* New Light.) "The shining of the light," or doctrinal understanding, it declares, "has been progressive, just as the light of early dawn gives way to sunrise and the full light of a new day." Then it cites an alleged case in point:

> For example, in 1962 there was an adjustment of understanding regarding "the superior authorities" of Romans 13:1–7.
> For many years the Bible Students had taught that "the higher powers" (KJV) were Jehovah God and Jesus Christ. . . . Years later, a careful reanalysis of the scripture was made . . . As a result, in 1962 it was acknowledged that "the superior authorities" are the secular rulers . . .

What the *Proclaimers* book fails to tell readers here is that this was actually a return to the previously rejected interpretation, not something new as the book implies.

This fact can be documented in the *Proclaimers* book on pages 189–190, where an unrelated discussion in a different chapter (perhaps by a different contributing author, though contributors are left unnamed) inadvertently acknowledges that "in the period leading up to World War I . . . At that time they understood that 'the higher powers,' referred to at Romans 13:1–7 (KJV), were the secular rulers"—the same conclusion they supposedly *reached in 1962 as new light.*

Holidays

While it is widely known that Jehovah's Witnesses abstain from exchanging Christmas gifts, few outsiders realize they believe it wrong to celebrate *any* of the holidays appearing on the calendar—even such apparently innocent occasions as Mothers Day and Thanksgiving. JWs have a separate argument prepared for each different holiday. In the case of the latter two, for example, they associate Mothers Day with a demon goddess and mother worship, and they believe that offering thanks to God on a day non-JWs set aside for Thanksgiving would constitute interfaith or spiritual adultery.

It is usually pointless to argue with individual Witnesses over holidays. As long as they view the Watchtower Society as God's mouthpiece, they will reject the holidays, regardless of how effective your argument may be. However, once other information has given them a more balanced view of the Brooklyn-based organization, they will be ready to rethink their position on holidays. So, the information presented here is not intended for use as an opening argument when initiating discussions. Rather, it will prove helpful later when a JW you are helping is leaving the organization and must wrestle with the issues involved. Also it will help non-Witnesses see the holes in arguments JWs advance against holiday observances.

The basic reason why the Watchtower Society's wholesale ban on all holidays is wrong is that it is not biblical. It contradicts Romans 14:5 and 6, which says in the JW *New World Translation*: "One man judges one day as above another; another man judges one day as all others; let each man be fully convinced in his own mind. He who observes the day observes it to Jehovah." *The Jerusalem Bible* renders the same verse this way: "If one man keeps certain days as holier than others, and another considers all days to be equally holy, each must be left free to hold his own opinion. The one who observes special days does so in honor of the Lord." So Paul told the Romans that a Christian should be free to celebrate the Jewish holy days or holidays if he or she chose to do so. But a JW who celebrates those days today is disfellowshiped, in complete disregard for what Romans 14 says. A JW who holds a special meal on Christmas or Easter to honor Christ can be expelled from the organization.

If you find yourself discussing holidays with a Jehovah's Witness, a word of caution is in order. Avoid falling into the trap of trying to defend *every* holiday and *every* method of celebrating. Our recognizing that the Watchtower ban on all holidays goes "beyond what is written" (1 Corinthians 4:6 NIV, RSV) and is therefore wrong does not mean that we should go to the opposite extreme and automatically assume that every holiday is okay—or that if a holiday itself is acceptable then absolutely any method of celebration is acceptable. We need not put our stamp of approval, for example, on Halloween or on days various nations set aside to honor their national heroes or to rejoice over victories in territorial battles. Nor should we feel obligated to defend lavish spending or drunken parties that some people indulge in with a holiday as their excuse. Romans 14 speaks of holidays that "honor the Lord."

See also Christmas *and* Birthdays.

Holy Spirit

Jehovah's Witnesses deny both the deity and the personality of the Holy Spirit. To them "it" is simply an impersonal force that God uses to accomplish his will—reminiscent of the Force spoken of by characters in the Hollywood motion picture *Star Wars* who blessed one another by saying, "The Force be with you!" The JW *New World Translation* generally omits capitalization and instead employs the expression "holy spirit" without the definite article. In Genesis 1:2 it says that "God's active force" was moving over the surface of the waters.

Still, in spite of such distortions, the *New World Translation* testifies to the personhood of the Holy Spirit. Its verses reveal that the Spirit speaks (Acts 13:2), bears witness (John 15:26), says whatever he hears (John 16:13), feels hurt (Isaiah 63:10), and so forth. Acts 5:3–4 reveals that lying "to the holy spirit" is the same as lying "to God." (How could someone lie to a "force"?)

However, only a translation that recognizes the personality and deity of the Holy Spirit can make sense of a passage like Romans 8:26–27,

> In the same way, the Spirit helps us in our weakness. We do not know what we ought to pray for, but the Spirit himself intercedes for us with groans that words cannot express. And he who searches our hearts knows the mind of the Spirit, because the Spirit intercedes for the saints in accordance with God's will. (Romans 8:26–27 NIV)

Telling his disciples he would soon be leaving them, Jesus comforted them with the knowledge that

> I will ask the Father, and he will give you another Counsellor to be with you for ever—the Spirit of truth. The world cannot accept him, because it neither sees him nor knows him. But you know him, for he lives with you and will be in you. (John 14:16–17 NIV)

Only another divine Person could take Christ's place like this pending his return. Unfortunately, Jehovah's Witnesses "cannot accept him" because, like the world, they "neither see him nor know him."

Interestingly, Charles Taze Russell coauthored the book *Three Worlds, or Plan of Redemption* with Nelson H. Barbour in 1877, two years before Russell began independently publishing his own *Watch Tower* magazine. This book defends the trinitarian view of the Holy Spirit as a Person, attacking Christadelphians for deviating from this:

> I am beginning to think Age-to-come people, and many others among pre-millennialists, do not believe in *anything* of a spiritual nature . . . or in the existence [*sic*] of spiritual beings, or even of the Holy Spirit itself. I *know* one class of age-to-come believers, the *Christadelphians*, do not. The Holy Spirit, say they, is but a principle, or element of power, and

not an intelligence. It is nothing more nor less than "electricity;" is taught in one of their books, now before me.

—*Three Worlds, or Plan of Redemption,*
pages 57–58

Perhaps Russell believed in the deity of the Holy Spirit at that time, or perhaps principal author N. H. Barbour's views prevailed over his own, but five years after the publication of *Three Worlds* Russell used several pages of the July, 1882, *Watch Tower* to present arguments against the personality of the Holy Spirit. Jehovah's Witnesses still do so today, representing "holy spirit" as a "force" like electricity, the same as the Christadelphians Russell joined in condemning.

For help in responding to JW misuse of specific Bible verses in regard to the Holy Spirit, please see my book *Jehovah's Witnesses Answered Verse by Verse.*

House to House Preaching

"We are the only ones preaching the Good News from door to door as Jesus and the apostles did." Jehovah's Witnesses often throw this in the face of Christians as evidence that theirs is the true religion. "We are the only ones fulfilling Jesus' words, 'And this gospel of the kingdom shall be preached in all the world for a witness unto all nations; and then shall the end come,'" they add. (Matthew 24:14 KJV) However, their argument is fatally flawed in two ways:

First of all, there is no biblical evidence that Jesus went from house to house. He preached in the synagogue, in the marketplace, on a mountain, at the seashore, at the temple—virtually anywhere people gathered—but no passage of Scripture shows him going up and down the street knocking on doors.

There are two verses JWs use to suggest that the apostles did door-to-door preaching: Acts 5:42 ("Day after day, in the temple courts and from house to house, they never stopped teaching and proclaiming the good news that Jesus is the Christ."—NIV) and Acts 20:20 ("You know that I have not hesitated to preach anything that would be helpful to you but have taught you publicly and from house to house."—NIV). In both verses, however, the expressions translated "from house to house" at Acts 5:42 can also mean "in every house" (KJV), "at home" (*American Standard Version*), "in private houses." (*The Twentieth Century New Testament*) The expression at Acts 20:20 is variously translated "in your homes" (Rotherham's *The Emphasized New Testament*), "in private" (*The Twentieth Century New Testament*), and "in homes." (William F. Beck's *The New Testament in the Language of Today*) Church buildings were unknown to the early Christian congregation, and local churches met in private homes. (Compare Philemon 2—"the church in thy house.")

Some door-to-door preaching may have taken place, but if this were as regular a feature of apostolic activity as it is with Jehovah's Witnesses today, there would no doubt be accounts of actual door-to-door experiences scattered throughout the New Testament. Scripture testifies against this, however, not only by the absence of such accounts, but also by the instructions Jesus gave when he sent out the seventy two by two; he commanded them specifically, "And in the same house remain, eating and drinking such things as they give: for the labourer is worthy of his hire. Go not from house to house." (Luke 10:7 KJV)

The second fatal flaw in the argument that door-to-door preaching identifies JWs as the true religion has to do with the message they deliver. Jesus said that "this gospel of the kingdom shall be preached" (Matthew 24:14), but Jehovah's Witnesses preach a gospel foreign to Christ and the apostles.

See Gospel.

142

Jehovah

Jehovah is the most commonly used English-language rendering of the Tetragrammaton, the name of God featured thousands of times in the Old Testament. It appears there as four Hebrew consonants *Yod He Vav He* (YHWH or JHVH) with vowel sounds to be supplied by the reader. Many authorities believe that *Yahweh* is closer to the original pronunciation. The *King James Version* Bible substitutes LORD with small caps in most places where the Tetragrammaton appears—reflecting the later Jewish practice of saying *Adonai* (*Lord*) when reading aloud in fearful avoidance of voicing the sacred name—but the KJV spells out *Jehovah* in four places: Exodus 6:3; Psalm 83:18; Isaiah 12:2 and 26:4.

Jehovah's Witnesses misuse the name Jehovah in four ways:

(1) They teach that it "is wrong to *fail* to use that name." (*You Can Live Forever in Paradise on Earth*, page 44) For them it is one of the identifying marks of the true religion, so that any church or denomination that does not feature the name continually in its worship services and in its literature is automatically part of Satan's empire of false religion. The most obvious refutation for this is that such a standard would condemn Peter, Paul, John, and the other New Testament writers and the first century churches associated with them. There is no evidence that the apostles or the early Christians—particularly the Greek-speaking converts who quickly made up the majority of the early Church—attached any such special significance to the use of this name. Rather, congregations of believers were "assembled in the name of our Lord Jesus." (1 Corinthians 5:4 NIV) In seasons of persecution Christians were "insulted because of the name of Christ." (1 Peter 4:14) The apostles

143

taught "in the name of Jesus" and proclaimed that "there is no other name under heaven given to men by which we must be saved." (Acts 4:12, 18 NIV)

(2) Denying the deity of Christ and the personality and deity of the Holy Spirit, Witnesses apply the name *Jehovah* only to the Father. In doing so, however, they ignore the testimony of Scripture concerning the triune nature of God. Theological considerations aside, their own *New World Translation* testifies to the divine name's application to the Son ("Father, watch over them on account of your own name which you have given me"—John 17:11) and to the Holy Spirit ("Now Jehovah is the Spirit"—2 Corinthians 3:17).

(3) JWs believe that God requires us to use the name *Jehovah* when addressing him in prayer. (*See* Prayer.)

(4) Sect members see the very name "Jehovah's Witnesses" as proof that theirs is the one true religion. (*See* Jehovah's Witnesses.)

Jehovah's Witnesses

To members of the sect the designation "Jehovah's Witnesses" is no mere denominational name; rather, it identifies them as God's earthly witnesses to mankind. They believe that God gave them this name when he inspired Isaiah 43:10, "'YOU are my witnesses,' is the utterance of Jehovah . . ." (NWT)

In actuality it was Watchtower president Joseph Rutherford who selected the name. On July 26, 1931 he presented a resolution to assembled followers, asking them to approve the new name "Jehovah's Witnesses." Prior to that time they had referred to themselves as "Bible Students," whereas orthodox Christians called them "Russellites." Following the death of founder Charles Taze Russell, his successor J. F. Rutherford's authoritarian methods provoked a schism among the Bible Students, with some adhering to the Watchtower corporation while others formed competing groups. It was in an effort to distance his followers from the latter that Rutherford proposed the new name "Jehovah's Witnesses." He stated this reason for the new name in the resolution he asked his followers to adopt in 1931:

> WHEREAS shortly following the death of Charles T. Russell a division arose between those associated with him in such work, resulting in a number of such withdrawing from the Watch Tower Bible & Tract Society, and who have since refused to cooperate with said Society and its work and who decline to concur in the truth as published by the Watch Tower Bible & Tract Society, in *The Watch Tower* and the other recent publications of the above-named corporations, and have opposed and do now oppose the work of said Society in declaring the present message of God's kingdom and the day of the vengeance of our God against all parts of Satan's organization; and said opposing ones have formed themselves into divers and numerous companies and have taken and now bear such names as, to wit, "Bible Students," "Associated Bible Students," "Russellites teaching the truth as expounded by Pastor Russell," "Stand-Fasters," and like names, all of which tends to cause confusion and misunderstanding . . .
>
> —1931 booklet titled *The Kingdom, the Hope of the World* by J. F. Rutherford, pages 30–31

So, the selection of a new name was necessitated by the split in the Bible Student community some years earlier. Adoption of this new name repudiated the position Russell had set forth in the early days of the sect:

> We believe that a visible organization, and the adoption of some particular name, would tend to increase our numbers and make us more respectable in the estimation of the

world. . . . But . . . We always refuse to be called by any other name than that of our Head—Christians.

—*Zion's Watch Tower*, March, 1883, page 458, reprints

The JW position that the designation "Jehovah's Witnesses" is a God-given name identifying them as the true organization of God's people is untenable. Any group of people could likewise form a sect and name it "Jehovah's Congregation," "Church of God," "Disciples of Christ," and so on, with equal validity.

Jesus Christ

"Whoever told you that we don't believe in Christ must have been misinformed," a middle-aged Jehovah's Witness lady says in response to such an objection from a young woman she is visiting. "We most certainly do believe that Jesus Christ is the Son of God, and we accept him as our Lord and Savior."

What, then, is the problem? The problem is that the Witness says this not to put herself in agreement with orthodox Christianity, but merely to *appear* to be in agreement in order to disarm an opponent or to allay the fears of a prospective convert. In actuality, most of the significant words in her sentence have been so completely redefined for her by the Watchtower organization that she means something entirely different from what a Bible-believing Christian means when saying the same thing.

In the Witness lady's mind *Jesus Christ* is the incarnate name of Michael the archangel, he can be called *the Son of God* by virtue of being the first angel God created, he is *Lord* in the sense of holding the second-in-command position in God's heavenly organization, and he is *Savior* only partially because he opened the way for us to gain eternal life on earth and left it up to us to do the rest. So, when she said, "We most certainly do believe that Jesus Christ is the

Son of God, and we accept him as our Lord and Savior," what she actually meant was, "We believe that Michael the archangel was the first angel God created, and we accept him as second-in-command in God's organization—the one who opened the way for us to gain eternal life in an earthly paradise if we do all that the organization instructs us to do." This is a far cry from what orthodox Christians mean by the same words!

Although the *New World Translation* reduces Christ Jesus to "a god" at John 1:1, it still reveals him as God at John 20:28 ("In answer Thomas said to him: 'My Lord and my God!'" ᴺᵂᵀ) and at Isaiah 9:6 ("For there has been a child born to us, there has been a son given to us . . . And his name will be called Wonderful Counselor, Mighty God . . .").

When Christians point this out, Jehovah's Witnesses often respond that "the Mighty God is not the same as the Almighty God."

The Watchtower Society provides them this argument:

> Because of his unique position in relation to Jehovah, Jesus is a "Mighty God." —John 1:1; Isaiah 9:6 But does not "Mighty God" with its capital letters indicate that Jesus is in some way equal to Jehovah God? Not at all. Isaiah merely prophesied this to be one of four names that Jesus would be called, and in the English language such names are capitalized. Still, even though Jesus was called "Mighty," there can be only one who is "Almighty." To call Jehovah God "Almighty" would have little significance unless there existed others who were also called gods but who occupied a lesser or inferior position.
> —*Should You Believe in the Trinity?*,
> page 28

Notice, however, that even in the *New World Translation* Isaiah 9:6 does not really say Jesus will be called "a" Mighty God as the Society says here, but rather that he will be called "Mighty God":

> For there has been a child born to us, there has been a son given to us; and the princely rule will come to be upon his shoulder. And his name will be called Wonderful Counselor, Mighty God, Eternal Father, Prince of Peace.

What about the rest of the Society's argument? It contradicts the Bible on three points:

(1) Just *how* mighty is Jesus Christ? Hebrews 1:3 says he is "upholding the universe by his word of power" (RSV) or "he sustains all things by the word of his power." (NWT) And at Matthew 28:18 Jesus himself says he has "*all* authority" (NW) or "*all* power . . . in heaven and in earth." (KJV)

(2) Who did Jeremiah understand the "mighty" God to be? Jeremiah knew this to be the one true "God, the great One, the mighty One, Jehovah of armies being his name."—Jeremiah 32:18 NWT

(3) Who did Isaiah himself mean by the expression "Mighty God"? Isaiah did not stop writing at Isaiah 9:6. He went on to say, ". . . and they will certainly support themselves upon Jehovah, the Holy One of Israel, in trueness. A mere remnant will return, the remnant of Jacob, to the Mighty God."—Isaiah 10:20, 21 NWT

So Jeremiah and Isaiah himself identify the mighty God as being the same as the Almighty God, Jehovah. This fits the fact that Jesus Christ has all authority, all power, all might, hence by definition is the Almighty God.

See Michael the Archangel, "God's Organization," New World Translation, *and* Salvation.

Justification

The Word of God tells believers, ". . . ye are justified in the name of the Lord Jesus, and by the Spirit of our God." (1 Corinthians 6:11 KJV) Since J. F. Rutherford introduced the idea back in 1935, however, the Watchtower Society has taught new converts to view themselves as a "great crowd" of "other sheep" not part of the new covenant mediated by Christ for only a "little flock" of 144,000 destined for heaven. The vast majority of JWs, then, have been taught that they do not receive the justification promised in the New Testament: "The 'great crowd' . . . will not be justified or declared righteous either now or then as the 144,000 heavenly joint heirs have been justified while still in the flesh."—*Life Everlasting-in Freedom of the Sons of God,* 1966, page 391

Recently, however, large numbers have left the Jehovah's Witness organization to embrace true Christianity, and these ex-JWs have been loudly pointing out the unscriptural nature of this "great crowd" doctrine. In the face of such pressure, the Society has recently begun to apply Christian terminology to the "great crowd," as follows.

> ". . . the 'great crowd' . . . Because of their faith in the Lamb's shed blood, a degree of righteousness is credited to them. . . . a relatively righteous standing . . . Like Abraham, they are accounted, or declared righteous as friends of God."
> —*The Watchtower,* December 1, 1985, page 17

So, the Society here credits "a degree of righteousness" to rank-and-file JWs. This, however, still appears to fall short of the full justification promised in the New Testament to all believers: "And by him all that believe are justified from all things, from which ye could not be justified by the law of Moses." (Acts 13:39 KJV) So, when the February 15, 1995 Watchtower states that "the great crowd" are "declared righteous as God's friends with a view to surviving the great tribulation"—language similar to that used in 1985 above—it is unclear whether this represents a further change in viewpoint or whether the qualifying expressions "a degree of righteousness" and "relatively righteous" are still held to apply to JWs with the earthly hope.

See Heaven, Great Crowd, Little Flock, *and* Other Sheep.

Kingdom of God

The Kingdom of God is very real to Jehovah's Witnesses because they see themselves as loyal subjects living under the rulership of a divine government represented on earth by the Watchtower Society. This is not a point that would be profitable for you to debate with JWs, but some understanding of how they view the Kingdom will give you insight into their thinking on many other matters.

God's Word tells Christians that "he has rescued us from the dominion of darkness and brought us into the kingdom of the Son he loves." (Colossians 1:13 NIV) To one degree or another we may view the local church as a manifestation of God's Kingdom, but our living under Kingdom rule is manifested primarily in our personal relationship with God. Christ is not only our Savior, but also our Lord, our Master, our King. When they came into conflict with governmental authorities attempting to restrict their preaching, "Peter and the other apostles replied: 'We must obey God rather than men!'" (Acts 5:29 NIV) Christians view Christ as the ultimate authority rightly laying claim to our obedience in everyday life.

With Jehovah's Witnesses, on the other hand, the Kingdom manifests itself as a complex governmental organization ruling right alongside the secular government. Ministry School instructors are its school teachers; elders are its town officers and policemen; "ministerial servants" are its bureaucrats; congregation judicial committees are its courts. Quick-build crews that erect new Kingdom Halls constitute its public works department. The local Kingdom Hall is its town hall, and the Watchtower Society's

Brooklyn headquarters complex is its White House, Supreme Court, and Capitol. JWs believe God to be the invisible Chief Executive in this "theocratic" government, but, like other self-proclaimed theocracies down through history, it is actually a human hierarchy that wields power.

Little Flock

The number of those who end up spending eternity in heaven with Christ is literally 144,000 according to Watchtower teaching—a small number from among the billions of humankind.

> "Jehovah has established a limited number, 144,000, to make up the little flock, and has been gathering it since Pentecost 33 C.E. . . . the general gathering of these specially blessed ones ended in 1935."
> —*The Watchtower*, February 15, 1995, page 19

The "little flock" is the group to whom Jesus spoke the words at Luke 12:32, "Do not be afraid, little flock, for your Father has been pleased to give you the kingdom." The context, however, indicates that Jesus was speaking to "his disciples" without mentioning a limited number. (Luke 12:22) When Peter asked, "Lord, are you telling this parable to us, or to everyone?" Jesus' response indicated that he was addressing all those who would prove faithful—again without fixing a definite number. (Luke 12:41–53 NIV) The JWs pull the number 144,000 from Revelation 7:4 and 14:1–3, a different context entirely.

You can refute the Watchtower's "little flock" doctrine by showing that Jesus set heaven as the goal for *all* believers. (*See* Heaven.) You might also ask a Jehovah's Witness to read Revelation 7:5–8, listing ". . . from the tribe of Reuben 12,000, from the tribe of Gad 12,000, from the tribe of Asher 12,000 . . ." and so on. Ask whether these are literal numbers. JWs believe each group of 12,000 to be figurative. How, then, can 12 figurative groups of 12,000 each add up to a literal 144,000?

See also Great Crowd *and* Other Sheep.

Marriage

Much like the Mormons, who use television advertisements to portray the Church of Jesus Christ of Latter-day Saints as a bastion of strong marriages and traditional family life, Jehovah's Witnesses commonly make similar claims for the Watchtower organization in their presentations on the doorstep. Listeners who have read about high divorce rates among churchgoers and who may know of marriage problems in their own church sometimes find it difficult to answer the claim that Jehovah's Witnesses have better marriages and happier family life. However, such hesitancy is solely due to unfamiliarity with the true facts about JW marriage and family life, not due to any real superiority of the Witnesses in this regard.

In actuality, JWs experience the same marriage problems as other people. During my eight years as an elder in a congregation with approximately a hundred active Witnesses, I repeatedly served on judicial committees hearing cases involving fornication, adultery, homosexuality, domestic violence, and so on. I recall specifically that we elders disciplined three couples who confessed to wife-swapping—an astounding number for a congregation of that size—but I early-on lost count of the individual acts of sexual immorality because there were so many. The September 15, 1987 *Watchtower* admits on page 13,

Unfortunately, during the 1986 service year, 37,426 had to be disfellowshipped from the Christian congregation, the greater number of them for practicing sexual immorality.

And this does not include the even higher number reproved for immorality but not disfellowshipped because they were sincerely repentant.

Moreover, beyond the weaknesses of the flesh common to people everywhere, there are additional unique factors producing marital and family problems among Jehovah's Witnesses.

For example, unlike Mormons who are encouraged by their religion to marry and bear children, Jehovah's Witnesses are actually discouraged from both, although not as strongly today as in the past. The teaching is based on the leadership's interpretation of Jesus' words about men who become "eunuchs for the kingdom of heaven's sake" (Matthew 19:12) and Paul's discussion of the pros and cons of marriage and singleness in 1 Corinthians, chapter 7. When the disciples winced at Christ's prohibition of frivolous divorce and answered Him, "If the case of the man be so with his wife, it is good not to marry," Jesus responded, "All men cannot receive this saying, save they to whom it is given." (Matthew 19:10–11) The Watchtower Society, however, has gone beyond Jesus' words about the gift of celibacy and Paul's balanced discussion of the alternatives, and has even gone so far as to present marriage as a course that is not "proper" for Christians:

Would it be Scripturally proper for them to now marry and begin to rear children? No, is the answer which is supported by the Scriptures.
—1938 booklet *Face the Facts*, page 46

During the late 1930s and early 1940s the admonition to remain single was promoted vigorously, and as a result many young Witnesses followed it. Those who wanted to marry were encouraged to "wait a few years, until the fiery storm of Armageddon is gone." (*Face the Facts*, page 50)

Many Witnesses who were strong in their faith followed this counsel and remained single so as to devote their time and energies to the preaching work. I met personally some of these unmarried full-time "pioneers" who were advancing in age at the time when I was in the organization (1969–82). Some of them seemed to have found fulfillment in celibate, full-time service, or at least that was the image they projected for public consumption. Others, it was plain to see, spent their final years lonely and bitter.

"Is This the Time To Have Children?" was the title of an article in *Awake!* magazine of November 8, 1974, which climaxed with this observation (page 11):

> Today there is a great crowd of people who are confident that a destruction of even greater magnitude is now imminent. The evidence is that Jesus' prophecy will shortly have a major fulfillment, upon this entire system of things. This has been a major factor in influencing many couples to decide not to have children at this time. They have chosen to remain childless so that they would be less encumbered to carry out the instructions of Jesus Christ to preach the good news of God's kingdom earth wide before the end of this system comes.

My wife Penni and I were among the "many couples" who made that decision to remain childless. Instead of rearing sons and daughters, we devoted extra hours to offering Watchtower literature from door to door and to conducting studies with potential converts. We produced "spiritual children" in this way, but most of them remained behind with the "mother organization" when we left in 1982.

The leaders who initiated and promoted such teachings were men who had serious problems of their own when it came to dealing with women. Watchtower founder Charles Taze Russell lived his final twenty years estranged from his wife Maria, who had battled him in divorce court for five years, eventually securing alimony. Russell died childless. His successor Joseph Franklin Rutherford managed to avoid the negative publicity of a messy divorce; after fathering a son named Malcolm, he simply lived apart from his wife Mary. When the Society alluded to this on page 85 of its 1993 book *Jehovah's Witnesses—Proclaimers of God's Kingdom*, it was the first time most JWs ever heard that Rutherford even had a family at all:

> Brother Rutherford was survived by his wife, Mary, and their son, Malcolm. Because Sister Rutherford had poor health and found winters in New York (where the Watch Tower Society's headquarters were located) difficult to endure, she and Malcolm had been residing in southern California, where the climate was better for her health.

There was an elderly Witness in my home congregation who took me under his wing when I was a new convert and gave me my first set of the Society's old books plus some 78-RPM records of J. F. Rutherford's talks. This longtime JW I'll call him "Jack" here to protect the privacy of his surviving family members—used to delight in quoting from Rutherford's talks he had heard discouraging young men from marriage. The Society's president encouraged them to remain single and pursue full-time service rather than get married, Jack would tell me, quoting Rutherford's description of a woman as "a hank of hair and a bag of bones." (Borrowing from an expression in a poem by Rudyard Kipling, "Judge" Rutherford said this before an audience of thousands at the 1941 Watchtower convention in St. Louis, Missouri.) "Jack" used to torment his wife by reciting that quote and then singing, "I wish I was single again."

The leadership's tendencies toward misogyny continued in the person of Frederick W. Franz, who became the sect's chief theologian after Rutherford's death and later its fourth president. Fred Franz never married. In 1992 he died a ninety-nine-year-old bachelor.

Most Witnesses though, even during the decades when marriage was frowned upon heavily, took wedding vows anyway, bore children, and then labored under a burden of guilt, always trying to compensate for these manifestations of "spiritual weakness." Some succeeded in postponing marriage for years, eventually taking a mate late in life. Third Watchtower president Nathan Knorr was an example of this. Born in 1905 and baptized a JW at the age of 18, he remained celibate until his forty-seventh year. His marriage at that time, when he was president of the Society, opened the way for others to follow suit and brought a softening of the organization's stance, but the teaching that singleness was the preferred course remained in place.

Another source of marriage problems among Jehovah's Witnesses has been the hierarchy's tendency to peer into bedroom intimacies. For example, the December 1, 1972 *Watchtower* magazine published an official policy that ruled off-limits certain forms of contact between husband and wife. The article said "the elders should act to try to correct the situation" if any of the forbidden practices "are brought to their attention" and authorized them to expel violators from the congregation (page 735). As soon as this information was published, JWs began approaching their local elders to confess imagined wrongs or to verify whether their conduct in bed had the Society's stamp of approval. Conscience-stricken women began reporting their husbands for touching them improperly during foreplay or intercourse, and elders began summoning husbands to judicial hearings on the matter. Couples under cross-examination were forced to discuss with the elders the most intimate details of their loveplay.

In his book *Crisis of Conscience* former Governing Body member Raymond Franz devotes several pages (42–48) to explaining how the matter was handled at Brooklyn head-quarters, where a considerable volume of correspondence and phone calls came in and went out over a period of years as elders and married couples submitted lovemaking techniques for approval. Franz also testifies to the anguish individuals underwent in the process and to the resulting broken marriages that were unable to hold up under this invasion of privacy—especially in cases involving a non-Witness husband suddenly finding his wife's coreligionists turning a spotlight on his most private moments.

Other *Watchtower* articles have since modified the organization's stand, adjusting and fine-tuning its position on sexual intimacies, with each readjustment bringing with it a new wave of problems for the enforcing elders and the targeted couples. Yet JWs preaching their assigned sermons on the doorstep continue to mouth the official claim that Jehovah's Witnesses succeed where others fail in maintaining happy marriages.

Michael the Archangel

The Watchtower says, "Jesus Christ further deserves honor because he is Jehovah's chief angel, or archangel." (*The Watchtower*, February 1, 1991, page 17) Jehovah's Witnesses believe the Son of God to be "Jesus Christ, whom we understand from the Scriptures to be Michael the archangel. . . ." (*The Watchtower*, February 15, 1979, page 31) Does that understanding really come "from the Scriptures"? Or is it, rather, a teaching that Watchtower leaders superimpose on Scripture?

God's inspired Word mentions Michael five times: as "one of the foremost princes" (Daniel 10:13 NWT), as "the prince of [Daniel's] people" (Daniel 10:21 NWT), as "the great prince who is standing in behalf of the sons of [Daniel's] people" (Daniel 12:1 NWT), as "the archangel" who "had a difference with the devil and was disputing about Moses' body" but "did not dare to bring a judgment against him in abusive terms" (Jude 9 NWT), and as a participant in heavenly conflict when "Michael and his angels battled with the dragon" (Revelation 12:7 NWT). Does one of these verses say that Michael the archangel is Jesus Christ? No. It is necessary to read Scripture *plus* a Watchtower argument to reach that conclusion.

That argument is presented this way in the April 15, 1991, *Watchtower* magazine, on page 28:

> Why do we conclude that Jesus is the archangel Michael?
> God's Word mentions only one archangel, and it speaks of that angel in reference to the resurrected Lord Jesus: "The Lord himself will descend from heaven with a commanding call, with an archangel's voice and with God's trumpet." (1 Thessalonians 4:16) At Jude 9 we find that this archangel's name is Michael.

The argument consists of three parts that can be analyzed separately: (1) "God's Word mentions only one archangel," (2) "it speaks of that angel in reference to the resurrected Lord Jesus," and (3) "this archangel's name is Michael."

In answer to (1) and (3) it should be noted that the term "archangel" is found only twice in the Bible—at 1 Thessalonians 4:16 and Jude 9—providing insufficient information to say for certain that there are no other archangels besides Michael. Although he is the only archangel *named* in Scripture, Michael is referred to as *"one of* the foremost princes." (Daniel 10:13 NWT) The Bible leaves open the possibility that there are other unnamed archangels besides Michael.

As for part (2) of the Watchtower argument, it is faulty logic to conclude that descending "with an archangel's voice" means that Jesus *is* an archangel. If descending with an archangel's voice makes Christ an archangel, then descending "with God's trumpet" makes Him God. The same logic must be applied to the entire verse, not just part of it.

Does the Bible teach anywhere else that Jesus Christ is a mere angel? On the contrary, the entire first chapter of Hebrews was written to show the *superiority* of the Son of God as compared with angels. "For example, to which one of the angels did he ever say: 'You are my son; I, today, I have become your father'?" (Hebrews 1:5 NWT) ("For God never said to any angel, 'Thou art my Son . . .'"—*New English Bible*) The Son is "the reflection" of the Father's glory "and the exact representation of his very being, and he sustains all things by the word of his power." (Hebrews 1:3 NW)

Angels consistently refuse to accept worship, saying: "Be careful! Do not do that! . . . Worship God." (Revelation 22:8–9 NWT) But, the Father's command concerning the Son is, "let all God's angels worship him." (Hebrews 1:6 NWT, edition of 1961) In a later edition of its Bible the Watchtower Society changed *worship* to *obeisance* at Hebrews 1:6. Still, regardless of how it is translated, the same Greek word *proskuneo* is used at both Revelation 22:8–9 and Hebrews 1:6. The *proskuneo* (worship or obeisance) that angels refuse to accept, but say to give only to God, is the same *proskuneo* (worship or obeisance) that the Father commands to be given to the Son at Hebrews 1:6.

Persons who stop following the man-made Watchtower organization and start following Jesus Christ soon come to appreciate that the Son of God is no mere angel. This realization is important, in order that they may "honor the Son just as they honor the Father." (John 5:23 NWT)

Military Service

Some persons are attracted to Jehovah's Witnesses by their abstinence from war, and the Witnesses themselves herald their "neutrality" as proof that they are the one true religion. The chapter "Identifying the True Religion," in their book *You Can Live Forever in Paradise on Earth* presents the argument this way (pages 189–190):

> Jesus said: "By this all will know that you are my disciples, if you have love among yourselves." (John 13:35) Do the religious organizations with which you are acquainted have this love? What do they do, for example, when the countries in which they live go to war against one another?
>
> You know what usually happens. At the command of worldly men the members of the various religious organizations go out on the battlefield and slaughter their fellow believers of another country. Thus Catholic kills Catholic, Protestant kills Protestant . . . How do Jehovah's Witnesses measure up in this matter of showing love to one another? They do not follow the course of worldly religions. They do not slaughter fellow believers on battlefields.

Does this argument really prove that Jehovah's Witnesses are the only true Christians, the only ones who "have love among themselves"? How should Christians answer JWs on this issue?

First, it is important not to let the Watchtower Society back us into a corner, making us feel that we need to defend every war ever fought or every church member who ever picked up a gun or a sword. Much of the warfare carried on by mankind—including those who call themselves Christians—has truly been indefensible. And we should not feel obligated to defend it.

It is helpful to remember how Jesus responded when His enemies tried to "catch him in his words" and asked Him, "Is it right to pay taxes to Caesar or not? Should we pay or shouldn't we?" (Mark 12:13–17 NIV) A *yes* answer would have angered the Jews who hated Roman domination, while a *no* answer would have angered the authorities and other Jews allied with them. Rather than let them trick him into answering *yes* or *no*, Jesus gave them a reply they had not expected and that neither side could argue with: "Whose image and inscription is this? . . . Pay back Caesar's things to Caesar, but God's things to God." (Mark 12:14–17 NWT)

So, rather than feel compelled to defend whatever Jehovah's Witnesses oppose, we may freely acknowledge that war is evil. It was evidently to Christians that James wrote, rebuking them, "What causes wars and what causes fightings among you? . . . You desire and do not have; so you kill. And you covet and cannot obtain; so you fight and wage war." (James 4:1–2 RSV)

We can further acknowledge that men and nations have wrongly claimed God's backing in wars that were mere selfish territorial disputes. However, we should point out that Jehovah's Witnesses are not the only ones who condemn war and abstain from participation in it. Conscientious objectors to military service have traditionally been found among Quakers, Mennonites, Seventh-Day Adventists, Brethren and, to a lesser extent, among certain Baptists. So, an individual with strong feelings against war is by no means forced to follow the Watchtower Society. There are many other alternatives.

What, though, about military service itself? Is it biblically condemned?

The Bible is full of accounts of godly persons waging war. Abraham led a small army, defeated kings, and rescued his nephew Lot. Joshua led the armies of Israel in the conquest of the Promised Land. David, "a man after God's own heart" (1 Samuel 13:14 KJV, RSV), was a warrior all his life. Even Christ, at his return, is shown leading heavenly armies in a devastating attack on the forces of evil.

A Jehovah's Witness would object, saying that all of the above-mentioned were waging righteous warfare. God was on their side. What is wrong, the Witnesses say, is to serve in a secular army.

Does the Bible prohibit Christians from serving in the armies of the nations? It is not our purpose here to answer the question of how far a Christian ought to go in obedience to military authority. After the war crimes trial of Adolf Eichmann, most commentators concluded that there are times when any soldier should stop "obeying orders." Moreover, Christians have debated for centuries how to define a "just war," or whether such a thing exists at all. Each Christian must prayerfully decide where to draw the line between obedience to men and conscience toward God. Although the *Watch Tower* magazine once admitted that "there is no command in the Scriptures against military service." (August 1, 1898, page 231, in Society's reprints page 2345) the organization in more recent times has let its young men know that they face severe disciplinary action—amounting to expulsion from the group—if they join the military. Even draftees who report for noncombatant "alternative service" work in a civilian hospital are punished by shunning. Is this Watchtower policy biblical?

The New Testament does not specifically address the question of military service for Christians, but it does mention persons who served in the Roman army. For example, when John the Baptist preached in territory under Roman occupation, "Soldiers also asked him, 'And we, what shall we do?' And he said to them, 'Rob no one by violence or by false accusation, and be content with your wages.'" (Luke 3:14 RSV) He could easily have told them to lay down their weapons and take off their uniforms, but he did not.

Jehovah's Witnesses will not accept for baptism a man in uniform. He must first obtain a discharge from the military before he can be baptized. But the apostle Peter freely baptized "a Roman army officer, Cornelius, a captain of an Italian regiment." (Acts 10:1 *Living Bible*) Since the JWs would refuse to baptize such a man, it is clear that they "overstep the commandment of God because of their tradition," teaching "commands of men as doctrines." (Matthew 15:3, 9 NWT)

While some other religious groups have gone against Christian principles by actually stirring up war fever and recruiting young men to fight for dubious causes, this does not leave Jehovah's Witnesses as the only true religion by default. Rather, by going "beyond what is written" in the opposite direction, Watchtower leaders have shown themselves to be equally unwilling to accept the direction of God's Word the Bible in this matter. (1 Corinthians 4:6) Far from identifying them as the only true religion, the shunning of young men whose conduct is not condemned in Scripture proves that Jehovah's Witnesses obey men rather than God. Although the men to whom they give unquestioning allegiance are their own organizational leaders rather than military or government leaders, their course is still one of unfaithfulness to God.

Mind Control

Speaking to "the millions of non-Witnesses who are studying the Bible with the Witnesses or who have studied with them at one time or another," the February 15, 1994 *Watchtower* asks rhetorically, "Were there any attempts to brainwash you? Did the Witnesses employ mind-control techniques on you?" *The Watchtower* answers for them: "'No' would doubtless be your frank response. Obviously, if these methods had been used, there would be an overwhelming number of victims . . ."

As a matter of fact, there *are* countless victims who have testified to Watchtower mind control in radio and TV interviews, in law courts, and in print. The non-religious book

Combatting Cult Mind Control (Rochester, VT: Park Street Press, 1988) by exit-counselor Steven Hassan deals mainly with "Moonies" but lists Jehovah's Witnesses among the cults and refers readers to books by former Witnesses that feature such personal testimony of Watchtower mind control victims.

Because it is implemented much more slowly than in many other cults, the Watchtower Society's program of mind control often goes unrecognized except by experts. Nevertheless, it shares basic elements with other "brainwashing" programs: (1) repetitive instruction, with books, magazines, and meetings all hammering home the same information, (2) new members told to break ties with outside friends and limit fellowship with non-member relatives, (3) a ban on reading critical works, (4) denunciation and shunning of ex-members, (5) verbal attacks undermining the authority of all outside institutions—religious, educational, medical, governmental, (6) a unique vocabulary with "loaded" language reinforcing the sect's rules, and (7) an orchestrated superiority/inferiority-guilt complex. Former members who have not been deprogrammed commonly report problems with anxiety, fear, and disorientation, as well as difficulty reintegrating into society at large—symptoms often associated with victims of mind control.

See Censorship *and* Shunning.

Minister(s)

"Good morning! We are ministers visiting our neighbors to share some important information from the Bible." These words might be expected from two middle-aged men in business suits, but the same introduction recited by an 8-year-old boy clinging to his mother's side tends to raise eyebrows. Though Jehovah's Witnesses call anyone who participates in their door-to-door literature distribution program a *minister,* most of the households visited employ the term more restrictively to designate a clergy-man, especially one who pastors a congregation.

Jehovah's Witnesses are entitled to redefine the word if they wish, of course, though it would make more sense for them to use such language among themselves than in con-versation with outsiders. The difference is merely a mat-ter of semantics, and not a point worth arguing about at the doorstep. However, the fact that JW leaders have argued about it among themselves, with resulting flip-flops in the sect's teachings, is a point worth raising. Why? Because it helps prove that the Watchtower Society is not "God's organization."

A long history of doctrinal changes and failed prophe-cies is sufficient proof for most people, but JWs have been taught to dismiss past errors with the thought that "the light keeps getting brighter" as God provides progressive enlightenment. (*See* New Light.) In this matter of "minis-ters," however, the organization cannot claim that the changes in teaching have been progressive with advanc-ing light, for the simple reason that JWs ended up believ-ing the same way they had originally.

In essence, the changes took place along these lines: first, the official view was that all JWs were ministers; then the Society declared that only its appointed congregational leaders (elders and servants) were ministers, offering bib-lical support for this position; finally, it returned to teach-ing the original view.

These back-and-forth changes can be traced in the name changes of the Society's internal publication for those going door to door. The monthly was named *Kingdom Ministry* in 1956, because the Society taught that all JWs were ministers. In 1976 this teaching was reversed, so that only those appointed as elders, servants, and so on, were called ministers, and the members in general were not ministers. So, in 1976 the publication's name was changed

165

to *Our Kingdom Service.* Then in 1982 after a shakeup on the Governing Body involving expulsion of Raymond Franz from the organization, the teaching was reversed again—back to the earlier point of view—and the term ministers was again applied to all active Witnesses. Accordingly, the publication's name was changed again, this time to the present form, *Our Kingdom Ministry.* Illustrations and text on page 247 of the JW book *Jehovah's Witnesses—Proclaimers of God's Kingdom* purportedly covering the history of this internal publication show earlier and current versions of the monthly but omit the 1956–76 *Kingdom Ministry* and the 1976–82 *Our Kingdom Service*—evidently to hide the facts about this embarrassing back-and-forth doctrinal flip-flop.

New Light

Ask a Jehovah's Witness, "What do you learn from the fact that your organization changed its teaching on flags and military service, used to view the Great Pyramid as 'God's Stone Witness,' banned vaccinations and organ transplants, changed its mind on Christmas, and predicted events for 1914, 1925, and 1975 that failed to come true?"

The Witness is likely to answer, "I learn from those past errors that this *really is* God's organization. The fact that we no longer adhere to those false teachings proves that God keeps making our light get brighter. It proves that God is leading this organization."

At this point in their dialogue with a Jehovah's Witness many Christians simply throw up their hands. What else can you do with people who see a whole string of past errors as proof that their organization is "the truth"?

Yes, the "new light" argument is a clever shield the Watchtower Society uses to plead *not guilty* in one situation after another. It is the equivalent of a child answering back, "What I said before doesn't count, because I had my fingers crossed." This religious *king's X* loses its power, however, when examined more closely.

The idea is based on an interpretation of Proverbs 4:18 which reads, "But the path of the righteous ones is like the bright light that is getting lighter and lighter until the day is firmly established." (NWT) In context this is not a justification for doctrinal changes at all, but rather a contrast with "the path of the wicked." (verse 14) "The way of the wicked is as darkness: they know not at what they stumble." (verse 19) The context fails to justify the interpretation JWs place on verse 18.

Essential to the JW theory of "light getting brighter" is the obvious requirement that any light *from God* must be true, regardless of whether it is old light or new light, since Jesus Christ is "the way, *the truth,* and the life." (John 14:6) Watchtower founder Charles Taze Russell acknowledged this shortly after he left the Adventist group he had been associated with and started his own religious magazine. The Adventists had always been coming up with "new light" to explain prophetic failures and other changes in beliefs. Russell's new magazine denounced that practice. It said:

> If we were following a man undoubtedly it would be different with us; undoubtedly one human idea would contradict another and that which was light one or two or six years ago would be regarded as darkness now; But with God there is no variableness, neither shadow of turning, and so it is with *truth;* any knowledge or light coming from God must be like its author. A new view of truth never can contradict a former truth. *"New light"* never extinguishes older *"light,"* but adds to it.
> —*Zion's Watch Tower,* February 1881, page 3

Russell published that statement less than two years after starting his magazine. In subsequent years, however, the Watchtower Society he founded has gone on to outdo the Adventists in proclaiming contradictory "new light." After teaching for nearly fifty years that the Great Pyramid of Egypt was God's stone witness and prophet, it turned about to label the Pyramid "Satan's Bible." (*See* Pyramid.) After encouraging followers to celebrate Christmas, it went on to forbid observance of the holiday. (*See* Christmas.) After declaring that Christ returned in 1874 and was "present" since then, it came up with new calculations and changed the date to 1914. (*See* Presence.) In each case the "new light" contradicted the "old light," demonstrating that it could not be from God.

A divine source could also be ruled out if it could be shown that the sect taught one thing, abandoned that teaching as false in view of "new light," but then returned once again to the old teaching and resumed teaching it. Pointing the finger at others for acting that way, *The Watchtower* of May 15, 1976, made this observation:

> It is a serious matter to represent God and Christ in one way, then find that our understanding of the major teachings and fundamental doctrines of the Scriptures was in error, and then after that, to go back to the very doctrines that, by years of study, we had thoroughly determined to be in error. Christians cannot be vacillating—"wishy-washy"—about such fundamental teachings. What confidence can one put in the sincerity or judgment of such persons? [page 298]

Yet this is exactly what the Watchtower Society itself has done on a number of matters. It taught that the "higher powers" of Romans 13:1 that we must obey are the secular governments, then denounced this as false doctrine and identified the "higher powers" as God and Christ, and then, some years later, returned to the original viewpoint. (*See* Higher Powers.) It flip-flopped back and forth on the question of whether the men of Sodom would be resurrected. (*See* Resurrection.) The Society told its followers they were all "ministers," then denied this and told them instead that only the appointed leaders were ministers, and then later returned to the original position. (*See* Minister.) A similar back-and-forth shift occurred in the sect's teaching on the identity of the "faithful and wise servant" of Matthew 24:45. (*See* Faithful and Discreet Slave.)

Realizing that it can hardly claim progressive enlightenment from God while flip-flopping on doctrinal matters, the organization has gone so far as to deny that this has ever happened:

> At times explanations given by Jehovah's organization have shown adjustments, seemingly to previous points of view. But this has not actually been the case. This might be compared to what is known in navigational circles as "tacking." By maneuvering the sails the sailors can cause a ship to go from right to left, back and forth, but all the time making progress toward their destination in spite of contrary winds.
> —*The Watchtower*, December 1, 1981,
> page 27

The examples cited above, however, prove beyond doubt that the organization has indeed returned "to previous points of view" on a number of matters. Instead of "getting brighter" the Watchtower's light has actually been blinking on and off. Rather than "tacking into the wind," a more accurate description would be that given in the JW *New World Translation* of the Bible at Ephesians 4:14, ". . . tossed about as by waves and carried hither and thither by every wind of teaching by means of the trickery of men, by means of cunning in contriving error." The *Living Bible* paraphrases it this way: ". . . forever changing our minds about what we believe because someone has told us something different, or has cleverly lied to us and made the lie sound like the truth."

New World Translation

A high priority with Jehovah's Witnesses when conducting a "free home Bible study" with a new prospective convert is to replace the student's Bible—regardless of the version—with a copy of the *New World Translation of the Holy Scriptures* published by the Watchtower Bible and Tract Society. The constant pressure to distribute more of the products produced in the Society's huge factories constitutes only part of the motivation behind the desire that the new student acquire a JW Bible. The real driving force is the realization that it will be much easier to teach Watchtower doctrine using this unique translation. Why? Because hundreds of verses have been altered to facilitate that task.

For example, where other Bibles say that "the Spirit of God was moving over the face of the waters" (Genesis 1:2 RSV) their Bible reads "God's active force" instead of "the Spirit of God." This fits better with their belief that the Holy Spirit is an impersonal force. The Watchtower teaching that Jesus Christ is an angel is contradicted by the declaration of John 1:1 that "the Word was God." However, JW Bibles are changed here to say that "the Word was a god." (More on this, below.) Early editions of the *New World Translation* rendered Hebrews 1:6, "But when he again brings his First-born into the inhabited earth, he says: 'And let all God's angels worship him.'" This was acceptable, because the Society had been teaching that Christ should be worshiped. (*Make Sure of All Things*, 1953 edition, page 85) Later, after reversing this teaching, the Society eventually changed its Bible also, now making it read "And let all God's angels do obeisance to him."

While many translations render the tetragrammaton YHWH as LORD, others render it as Yahweh or Jehovah. This is appropriate in the Old Testament where this divine name actually appears in the original Hebrew. However, the Watchtower Society has gone beyond this, inserting the name Jehovah 237 times in the New Testament where it does not appear in Greek manuscripts. (Look at the word-for-word English that appears under the Greek text in the Society's own *Kingdom Interlinear Translation*. The name Jehovah is not there.)

Naturally, the Watchtower Society has many arguments to offer in support of its altered renderings. And these are convincing in the eyes of Jehovah's Witnesses, who view the organization as God's "channel of communication" and who are forbidden to read opposing literature. Independent scholars, on the other hand, recognize the *New World Translation* as doctrinally biased. (See *The Jehovah's Witnesses' New Testament* by Robert H. Countess, Presbyterian and Reformed Publishing Company, 1982 and 1987, page 93.)

Viewing all other translations as wrong and their own as the only correct one, Jehovah's Witnesses would be more likely to say that the *New World Translation* "corrects" verses that are mistranslated in other Bibles. However, when asked for the credentials of the men on the New World Bible Translation Committee, to verify whether they possessed the expertise that would qualify them to over rule traditional authorities on biblical languages, JWs reply that the identity of the translators remains confidential. Why? So that all credit will go to God rather than to men. The real reason for their anonymity was exposed in recent years when defectors who quit Watchtower headquarters identified the members of the Committee, revealing that none of them was expert in biblical Hebrew, Greek, or Aramaic—the original languages from which the Bible must be translated.

For many years Jehovah's Witnesses turned for support of their "a god" rendering of John 1:1 to *The New Testament* (1937) by Johannes Greber, since Greber also translated it, "the Word was a god." Watchtower Society publications quote or cite Greber in support of this and other renderings, as follows:

Aid to Bible Understanding (1969), pages 1134 and 1669

"Make Sure of All Things—Hold Fast to What is Fine" (1965), page 489

The Watchtower, September 15, 1962, page 554

The Watchtower, October 15, 1975, page 640

The Watchtower, April 15, 1976, page 231

"The Word"—Who Is He? According To John (1962),
      page 5

However, after ex-Witnesses gave considerable publicity to the fact that Greber was a spiritist who claimed that spirits showed him what words to use in his translation, *The Watchtower* of April 1, 1983, made this admission on page 31:

> This translation was used occasionally in support of renderings of Matthew 27:52, 53 and John 1:1, as given in the *New World Translation* and other authoritative Bible versions. But as indicated in a foreword to the 1980 edition of *The New Testament* by Johannes Greber, this translator relied on "God's Spirit World" to clarify for him how he should translate difficult passages. It is stated: "His wife, a medium of God's Spiritworld was often instrumental in conveying the correct answers from God's Messengers to Pastor Greber." *The Watchtower* has deemed it improper to make use of a translation that has such a close rapport with spiritism. (Deuteronomy 18:10–12) The scholarship that forms the basis for the rendering of the above-cited texts in the *New World Translation* is sound and for this reason does not depend at all on Greber's translation for authority. Nothing is lost, therefore, by ceasing to use his *New Testament.*

Here it appears that the Society has only just now discovered Greber's spiritistic connections and has immediately repented of using him for support. However, this, too, is yet another deception—because the JW organization already knew of Greber's spiritism back in 1956. *The Watchtower* of February 15, 1956, contains nearly a full page devoted to warning readers against Johannes Greber and his translation. It refers to his book titled *Communication with the Spirit-World: Its Laws and Its Purpose* and states, "Very plainly the spirits in which ex-priest Greber believes helped him in his translation." (*The Watchtower*, February 15, 1956, page 111)

Aside from Greber's *New Testament* and the Watchtower Society's slanted version, other English-language Bible translations are nearly unanimous in rendering John 1:1, "the Word was God." And this is consistent with the declaration by the Apostle Thomas, also found in John's Gospel, calling Jesus "My Lord and my God!" (John 20:28) Yes, the JW *New World Translation* still calls Jesus "God" at John 20:28 and Isaiah 9:6. In fact, their 1969 *Kingdom Interlinear* version reveals that the Greek literally says Jesus is "the God" (HO THEOS) at John 20:28.

See Bible, Deity, Jesus Christ, *and* God.

For additional information on the deity of Christ, and attempts by Watchtower translators to hide it in their Bible, see my book *Jehovah's Witnesses Answered Verse by Verse*.

Organ Transplants

The Watchtower Society now applauds surgical transplants as procedures that have "helped" people: "For the visually impaired, spectacles or contact lenses are often prescribed. Others have been helped by corneal transplants." (*Awake!*, August 22, 1989, page 6) Yet between 1967 and 1980 the Watchtower Society taught its followers to refuse transplants as violations of God's law. (See *The Watchtower*, November 15, 1967, pages 702–704.) The June 8, 1968, *Awake!* magazine taught Jehovah's Witnesses to "consider all transplants between humans as cannibalism." (page 21)

During the 13 years from 1967 to 1980, Jehovah's Witnesses were required to choose blindness rather than a cornea transplant, and to die rather than submit to a kidney transplant. (A former elder interviewed in England said that he resigned after a woman in his congregation went blind in obedience to the organization's command.)

In 1980, the Watchtower Society made transplants an optional "matter for personal decision." (*Watchtower*, March 15, 1980, page 31) And now it admits that people are "helped" by transplants.

Few newer JWs are aware of the sect's history on this score. When presenting this information we might ask a Witness, "How wise is it to entrust one's spiritual well-being to an organization that has misrepresented God's law in such life-and-death matters?"

Other Sheep

All believers in God, according to Jehovah's Witnesses, fall into two groups: the "little flock" of Luke 12:32 and the "other sheep" of John 10:16. The "little flock" is made up of 144,000 individuals who became followers of Christ between the first century and the year 1935 when that number was completed; they are the only believers bound for heaven. (*See* Little Flock.) All other believers in the true God—including pre-Christian patriarchs and the vast majority of Jehovah's Witnesses today—are among the "other sheep" whose destiny is everlasting life on a paradise earth. (Those of the "other sheep" who are alive when God brings this wicked world to an end constitute the "great crowd" according to the sect's interpretation of Revelation 7:9. *See* Great Crowd.)

Christian Bible commentators have generally understood Christ's "other sheep" to be the future believers from among the Gentile nations who would be added to the "little flock" of Jewish disciples Jesus gathered during his earthly ministry. Speaking to the latter he said, "I have other sheep that are not of this sheep pen. I must bring them also. They too will listen to my voice, and there shall be one flock and one shepherd." (John 10:16 NIV) As the Gospel message found hearers among the Greeks, Romans, and other pagan nations, the early Church expanded to include both Jews and Gentiles, gathered into "one flock" under the "one shepherd," Christ.

To refute the JW interpretation of the "other sheep," it is sufficient to demonstrate that Christians are not divided into a small heavenly class and a "great crowd" with earthly hopes. (*See* Little Flock *and* Great Crowd.) But you may also point out that pre-Christian believers "were aliens and strangers on earth . . . longing for a better country—a heavenly one. Therefore God is not ashamed to be called their God, for he has prepared a city for them." (Hebrews 11:13 16 NIV) What city in a heavenly country was prepared for the patriarchs and prophets of old? Evidently, "the heavenly Jerusalem, the city of the living God." (Hebrews 12:22 NIV)

See Heaven.

Paradise

Since its release in 1982 the Watchtower Society's book *You Can Live Forever in Paradise on Earth* has been the primary study text for prospective new converts.* During its first fifteen months in print nearly 15 million copies were produced in 55 languages according to *The Watchtower* of January 1, 1984, page 28. As the book's title indicates, it introduces readers to the hope that draws millions of

---

*As this book went to press a new book titled *Knowledge That Leads to Eternal Life* was released to serve as a replacement introductory textbook.

people to become Jehovah's Witnesses—the hope of everlasting life in a beautiful earthly paradise.

Such a promise is certainly attractive, especially for men and women who have not come to enjoy a personal relationship with God through Jesus Christ. Not knowing anyone in heaven, why would they want to end up going there? In fact, coming face-to-face with God on his home turf can be a frightening thought for many. A subtropical paradise in an earth forever rid of poverty, sickness, and death proves more appealing to human nature. But is it truly biblical to proclaim this as the Christian hope?

The Greek word translated *paradise* appears three times in the New Testament—at Luke 23:43, 2 Corinthians 12:4, and Revelation 2:7—but Jehovah's Witnesses largely ignore the two later verses and instead hang their hope on Jesus' words to the dying criminal nailed up next to him, as these words appear in the JW *New World Translation*: "Truly I tell you today, You will be with me in Paradise." (Luke 23:43) This constitutes Christ's promise that the man would be resurrected more than two thousand years later to life on an earth transformed to a beautiful garden park, Jehovah's Witnesses believe.

Unfortunately, however, the meaning of the verse in the *New World Translation* is affected by the anonymous translators' choice to punctuate Luke 23:43 differently from the way it appears in most other Bibles. Placing the comma after the word "today" instead of before it, the NWT gives Jesus' words a unique twist. It has Jesus *speaking* "today" to the man about being with him in paradise some time in the future, whereas the customary rendering with the comma before the word "today" indicates that they *arrive* in paradise that very day. Since ancient Greek manuscripts do not feature any punctuation to break the sentence into two parts, the comma's location in English depends on the translator's understanding of what is meant.

Interestingly, the Watchtower Society's *Comprehensive Concordance of the New World Translation of the Holy Scriptures* lists dozens of passages where Jesus uses the expression "Truly I say to you" or "Truly I tell you." (The same Greek word is rendered both "say" and "tell.") Comparing these verses reveals that the Society's translators punctuated them consistently—except Luke 23:43. Why did they punctuate that one verse differently? Perhaps because to do otherwise would disprove the Watchtower Society's teaching that the dead go nowhere—that those who die cease to exist. Jehovah's Witnesses are taught that it would be impossible for the dying man to go to Paradise that day, because he went into nonexistence pending a future resurrection.

Logically, though, there would be no need for Jesus to use the word "today" to point out when he was speaking. Whenever we open our mouth to speak, we are speaking "today," and the fact is so obvious that we need not mention it unless making a contrast with something spoken on a different day. Here the context reveals nothing of that sort that would call for Jesus to verbalize the obvious fact that he was speaking "today." Rather, the only time factor under discussion was the matter of when Jesus would be in Paradise. The man dying next to him begged, "Jesus, remember me when you come into your kingdom." (Luke 23:42 NIV) Yes, Jesus would remember him. When? Today!

Moreover, it would be reasonable to assume that the Paradise Jesus spoke of as his destination after death would be the same Paradise that Revelation speaks of Christian overcomers going to: "He that hath an ear, let him hear what the Spirit saith unto the churches; To him that overcometh will I give to eat of the tree of life, which is in the midst of the paradise of God." (Revelation 2:7 KJV) According to the Watchtower Society's own publications, this verse speaks of a heavenly paradise, not an earthly one:

177

> "Hence, the reference here must be to the heavenly gardenlike realm inherited by these conquerors. There, 'in the paradise of God,' yes, in the very presence of Jehovah himself, these overcomers who have been granted immortality will continue to live eternally, as symbolized here by their eating of the tree of life."
>   —*Revelation—Its Grand Climax At Hand!*
>   page 37

The Apostle Paul likewise speaks of paradise as heavenly rather than earthly. At 2 Corinthians 12:2–4 he speaks of being "caught up into paradise" which he also calls "the third heaven."

Clearly, the earthly "paradise" Jehovah's Witnesses are promised by their organization and the heavenly "paradise" the Bible promises for Christians are not one and the same.

See also Heaven *and* Resurrection.

Patriotism

The Watchtower tells Jehovah's Witnesses that they "may not engage in politics nor get involved in violence between the nations; in fact, they may not even take part in nationalistic exercises." (December 1, 1981, page 23) The same issue of the magazine goes on to ridicule patriotism:

> One patriot even expressed it this way: "Our country! . . . may she always be in the right; but our country, right or wrong." But not so the Christian witnesses of Jehovah!
>   —page 30

Ironically, this statement appears in a discussion admonishing Witnesses to "serve loyally" with the Watchtower organization in spite of doctrinal flip-flops. (page 31) I recall that I was still a JW in good standing and was present in the audience at our local Kingdom Hall when this article was discussed using questions and answers during the Sunday morning *Watchtower* Study meeting. As clearly as if it were yesterday I recall a number of long-time members raising their hands to be called on by the study conductor, receiving the portable microphone, and relating their own testimonies of how they knew that certain former doctrinal teachings were wrong, but they stayed loyally with the organization anyway. The rest of the audience expressed approval of each one who stuck loyally with the organization, even when it was teaching or doing something wrong. So, when the study conductor reached the paragraph ridiculing patriots for saying, "our country, right or wrong," I raised my hand, waited to receive the microphone, and pointed out that we were in a poor position to condemn such patriots when we ourselves were advocating loyalty to our organization, right or wrong. People throughout the audience gasped. The study conductor disparaged my comment. I was never handed the microphone again. In fact, I stopped attending meetings and left the sect shortly afterward.

My point in relating that incident here is that Jehovah's Witnesses denounce others' patriotism while manifesting the same spirit themselves, only directed toward their organization instead of toward a secular government. In similar fashion they refuse to sing the national anthem of the nation where they reside, but they sing rousing songs hailing their own organization as a "holy nation" and declaring their "loyalty" to it. (*Sing Praises to Jehovah*, Songs 38 and 54) They refuse to recite the Pledge of Allegiance to the Flag, but they sing lyrics pledging to the organization "our steadfast allegiance." (Song 38)

I have profound respect for Quakers, Mennonites, and other sincere Christians who abstain from certain patriotic acts for reasons of conscience, but I fear that Jehovah's Witnesses have been hoodwinked into merely transferring

179

their patriotic loyalties from Washington, D.C. to Brooklyn, N.Y. (the location of Watchtower headquarters).

For other ways in which the JW organization manifests itself as a rival government, *see* Kingdom of God. *See also* Flags *and* Military Service.

Pleiades

The constellation Taurus in the night sky includes within its boundaries the Pleiades star cluster, of which six stars are visible to the naked eye in close formation. What does this have to do with Jehovah's Witnesses? For many years they believed the Pleiades to be God's heavenly home. Specifically, they identified the star Alcyone—the brightest one in the cluster—as the residence of Almighty God himself. (*See* Alcyone.) They believed Christ travelled there after his resurrection, and JWs expected to be transported through space to that star cluster to receive their heavenly reward. (*Watch Tower*, November 1, 1920, page 334)

As far back as 1895, *Zion's Watch Tower* expressed the belief that the visible universe revolves around the Pleiades as its center and "that that center may be the heaven of heavens, the highest heaven, the throne of God." (May 15, page 1814) Twenty years later the principal JW magazine was still saying, "the Pleiades may represent the residence of Jehovah, the place from which he governs the universe." (June 15, 1915, page 5710 Reprints)

Joseph F. ("Judge") Rutherford continued the pattern established by his predecessor Charles Taze Russell. In his 1928 book *Reconciliation* he taught that "the Pleiades is the place of the eternal throne of God." (page 14) In fact, the sect's leadership did not repudiate the idea until 1953 when *The Watchtower* declared that "it would be unwise for us to try to fix God's throne as being at a particular spot in the universe." (November 15, page 703)

The average Jehovah's Witness today is totally unaware that the organization ever taught such a thing. Researching the subject can be of tremendous shock value—forcing a JW to realize there may be more that he needs to learn about the organization he looks to for direction.

Politics

Consistent with their abstinence from voting in elections, Jehovah's Witnesses also refuse to hold public office. As support for their stand they cite Jesus' departure when a crowd wanted to make him king. (John 6:15)

In Jesus' case, however, there were issues involved that made his case quite different from that of someone elected or appointed to public office today. First of all, Jesus knew that he would soon rule as king in heaven with the entire earth included in his realm, so why accept a much smaller offer of kingship from men? Also, the men who wanted to make Jesus king were living under Roman rule. Their act would have constituted an act of treason in the eyes of the law rather than a legitimate political appointment.

Faithful godly individuals such as Daniel, Shadrach, Meshach, Abednego, Esther, Mordecai, and Nehemiah accepted political appointments to serve in high governmental positions in pagan secular states, evidently with divine approval. In the New Testament Paul's reference to Christians in "Caesar's household" is understood by many to include governmental rather than simply domestic service. (Philippians 4:22)

Politics has often been characterized as a dirty business, so it is certainly an area fraught with temptation and danger for Christians. Still, the examples above are sufficient to show that the Watchtower Society has gone beyond Scripture in ruling political officeholding off limits for its followers.

See also Voting.

Prayer

The Watchtower Society has taught its followers that they must address all their prayers to "Jehovah God," using this modern transliteration of the ancient Hebrew Tetragrammaton. (*You Can Live Forever in Paradise on Earth,* pages 44 and 228) However, is that what Jesus taught? The four Gospels record sufficient details of Jesus' earthly life for us to follow Him as our exemplar in the matter of prayer. Many of Jesus' prayers are recorded. Did He pray to "Jehovah God?" No, the pattern Jesus set is this:

> "Abba, Father, all things are possible to you."
> —Mark 14:36 NWT

> "Father, I thank you."
> —John 11:41 NWT

> "Father, the hour has . . ."
> —John 17:1 NWT

> "You must pray, then, this way: 'Our Father . . .'"
> —Matthew 6:9 NWT

The pattern Jesus set was to address God as "Father." In fact, even the *New World Translation* does not contain any examples of Christ praying to "Jehovah"—in spite of the fact that the name "Jehovah" is inserted by the translators in hundreds of verses.

Jehovah's Witnesses might object by saying, "Jesus had a close, special relationship with the Father. That's why He did not address Him as 'Jehovah.'" True, Jesus was in a close relationship with the Father, but his purpose was to bring *all* of His disciples into a close, special relationship with God, too. "No one comes to the Father except through me," Jesus taught. (John 14:6 NWT) Of Christians who come to the Father through Jesus, the Bible says, "you have received the Spirit of adoption by whom we cry out, 'Abba, Father.' The Spirit Himself bears witness with our spirit that we are children of God." (Romans 8:15, 16 NKJV)

How many of us grew up calling our earthly father "Francis" or "William" or "Ralph" or whatever his name may have been? Even if we were adopted, we learned to call him "Dad" or "Papa"—an intimate expression similar to "Abba, Father." Their insistence on using the name *Jehovah* instead reveals that Jehovah's Witnesses know God only from a distance.

Presence or *Parousia* of Christ

Are you eagerly awaiting Christ's Second Coming? Then you are being misled, because the Lord has already returned, according to Jehovah's Witnesses. A fundamental tenet of Watchtower theology is the claim that Christ returned invisibly around October 4 or 5 in the year 1914. Instead of the early disciples asking Christ "when shall these things be? and what shall be the sign of thy coming . . ." the *New World Translation* has them asking, "When will these things be, and what will be the sign of your presence . . . ?" (Matthew 24:3) The Watchtower Society interprets this alternative rendering as meaning an invisible return.

Few Jehovah's Witnesses are aware, however, that their organization originally taught that Christ returned forty years earlier, in 1874. This was one of Charles Taze Russell's main reasons for commencing publication of *Zion's Watch Tower and Herald of Christ's Presence* in 1879—he wanted to announce to the world that Christ had already returned and was then invisibly present. (Russell borrowed this teaching from his Adventist mentors. *See* Adventist Origins.) Later, after a number of prophecies predicting related events for the years 1914, 1918, and 1925—based on the 1874 date—proved false, the sect changed the time of Christ's return from 1874 to 1914. Actually, the teaching was changed back-and-forth over a period of nearly a decade, until the 1874 date was finally discarded in favor of 1914. For example, note the references to the two different dates in this series of quotes:

> The second coming of the Lord therefore began in 1874.
> —*Creation*, 1927, page 310 in early editions, page 289 in later editions

> If it is true that Jesus has been present since the year 1914, then it must be admitted that nobody has seen Him with his natural eyes.
> —*Golden Age*, 1930, page 503

> The conclusion must necessarily follow, and is supported by numerous scriptures, that the return of the Nobleman could not be before 1914, at which time the Kingdom began. . . . Prior to 1914 and years thereafter we thought that our Lord's return dated from 1874; and we took it for granted that the *parousia* or presence of our Lord dated from that time. An examination of the scriptures containing the word *parousia* shows that the presence of the Lord could not date prior to 1914.
> —*Golden Age*, 1934, pages 379, 380

> . . . Applying the same rule, then, of a day for a year, 1335 days after 539 A. D. brings us to 1874 A. D., at which time, according to Biblical chronology, the Lord's second presence is due.
> —*The Harp of God*, "5,736,190 Edition Printed March 1937," page 235

> It was in the year 1874, the date of our Lord's second presence, that the first labor organization in the world was created. From that time forward there has been a marvelous

increase of light . . . since 1874, as further evidence of the
Lord's presence since that date . . .
—*The Harp of God*, "5,736,190 Edition
Printed March 1937," page 240

In the year 1943 the Watch Tower Bible and Tract Society
published the book *"The Truth Shall Make You Free."* . . . This
moved forward the end of six thousand years of man's existence into the decade of the 1970's. Naturally this did away
with the year 1874 C.E. as the date of return of the Lord
Jesus Christ and the beginning of his invisible presence or
parousia.
—*God's Kingdom of a Thousand Years Has Approached*,
1973, pages 209, 210

So, it appears that the Society taught the 1874 date as "the
truth" for over fifty years, changed the date from 1874 to
1914 early in the 1930s, then went back to the 1874 date in
1937 in a new edition of *The Harp of God*, and finally
abandoned the 1874 date in 1943.

All of this confusion could have been avoided if, instead
of dabbling in prophetic speculation, the Society had
accepted the Bible's clear statements that Christ's return
will be both visible and unmistakable:

Wherefore if they shall say unto you, Behold, he is in the
desert; go not forth: behold, he is in the secret chambers;
believe it not. For as the lightning cometh out of the east,
and shineth even unto the west; so shall also the coming
of the Son of man be.
—Matthew 24:26–27 KJV

. . . every eye shall see him . . .
—Revelation 1:7

The doctrine that Christ returned invisibly in 1914 serves
as a foundation for many other Watchtower teachings,

including the leadership's claim to authority as Christ's representative on earth. When that foundation collapses, so does the entire structure built upon it.

See Chronology.

Pyramid

A stone pyramid measuring nine feet across its base with the name WATCH TOWER BIBLE AND TRACT SOCIETY engraved in large letters on its side dominates the landscape today off Cemetery Lane in the northern outskirts of Pittsburgh, Pennsylvania. It provides graphic evidence of the importance of Egyptian pyramids in the sect's early teachings—information that proves extremely unsettling to the few Jehovah's Witnesses who encounter it. It is very upsetting for them to face the fact that for some fifty years—under the presidencies of both Charles Taze Russell and Joseph Franklin Rutherford—the Watchtower Society employed pyramidology to foretell future events.

To understand this in the context of its times, it should be noted that the first western archeological expedition entered Egypt with Napoleon's invasion forces in 1798 and published its findings in a series of volumes appearing from 1809 through 1828. Shortly thereafter certain religious fringe groups in America began incorporating Egyptian artifacts into their belief structure, notably the Mormons with Joseph Smith's allegedly miraculous translation of "The Book of Abraham" from an Egyptian funereal text in 1835. More widespread interest in Egyptology developed in England and the United States immediately following 1882, when British military occupation of the territory made archeological sites more accessible. But even before that, in 1880, Mormon leader Orson Pratt was teaching about

> . . . a new witness that the Lord seems to have brought to light, by the opening of the Great Pyramid of Egypt. . . .

There seems to be a prophetic spirit running through the construction of all that vast superstructure, pointing forward to the very end. . . . Allowing one year to a cubit inch . . . This points out the very period of time when the Church was organized, and the very day and month and year. Sixty-one cubit inches are measured off, from that point . . . the generation that will close up the times of the Gentiles.
—Fiftieth Annual Conference Report of the Mormon Church, 1880, pages 86–87

These words of the Mormon Apostle were soon to be echoed by Charles Taze Russell in the third volume of his *Studies in the Scriptures*. He, too, saw prophetic wisdom in the ancient stone monument and included in that book a lengthy chapter titled, "The Testimony of God's Stone Witness and Prophet, the Great Pyramid in Egypt." In it he wrote

Call to mind that the full end of Gentile power in the world and the time of trouble which brings its overthrow, will be in the end of A.D. 1914. . . . Now we inquire, If the inches of the floor-lines of these passages represent a year, each, as claimed and admitted by Pyramid students, what date would these measures of the "Grand Gallery" indicate as the end of the high calling to the divine nature, which the "Grand Gallery" symbolizes? . . . this date, 1910, indicated by the Pyramid, seems to harmonize well with the dates furnished by the Bible. It is but four years before the full close of the time of trouble which ends the Gentile times; and when we remember the Lord's words—that the overcomers shall be accounted worthy to escape the severest of the trouble coming upon the world, we may well accept as correct the testimony of the Great Pyramid, that the last members of the "body" or "bride" of Christ will have been tested and accepted and will have passed beyond the vail before the close of A.D. 1910.
—*Studies in the Scriptures*, vol. 3, 1891 (1903 edition), pages 362–364

Unlike the Mormons who never made a major doctrinal issue of the Great Pyramid, Russell continued to promote it throughout his life, and even after his death through the pyramid-shaped monument he selected to be erected near his grave. This pyramid in Pennsylvania serves as a tourist attraction as well as a mute testimony to the religious roots of Jehovah's Witnesses:

> The Watch Tower Society burial lots in Rosemont United Cemeteries, five miles due north of Pittsburgh City, contain ample grave space for all the members of the Bethel family, and the Pilgrims and their wives—in all more than 275 adult graves. In the exact center of the Bethel lot will be erected diagonally the Pyramid Shape Monument as designed by Brother Bohnet, and accepted by Brother Russell as the most fitting emblem for an enduring monument on the Society's burial space. The size of this structure is nine feet across the base, and its apex stone is exactly seven feet above the ground surface level. It rests upon a concrete foundation five feet deep . . .
>
> —*Souvenir Report of the Bible Students Convention*, 1919, page 7

The name "WATCH TOWER BIBLE AND TRACT SOCIETY" is engraved in large letters on the pyramid's side, just below the wreathed cross and crown symbol used by the Society for many years. Close by the pyramid is a separate and much smaller headstone marking Russell's own grave. The headstone features his portrait and identifies him as "The Laodicean Messenger," a reference to the belief that he was "the messenger of the congregation in Laodicea" (Revelation 3:14 *Emphatic Diaglott*), that is, God's spokesman to Christians during the Laodicean period or phase of church history, in this dispensationalist view.

According to a January 10, 1986 article in a local newspaper, the *News Record*, which covers Pittsburgh's northern suburbs, "thousands" of people come "from all over the world" to photograph the Watch Tower Pyramid. "Russell felt the pyramids of Egypt had prophetic significance and used them extensively in his writing," the *News Record* went on to quote a Jehovah's Witness elder from the nearby Bellevue Congregation as saying. "They are not viewed that way any more by Jehovah's Witnesses," he added.

According to the *Watch Tower* magazine of May, 1881, pages 5–6,

> Thirty-three inches from the beginning of the grand gallery is a well, representing the death and resurrection of Jesus. From this well there is another downward passage-way which connects with the entrance passage near the pit, and seems to teach the restoration of all men from the "horrible pit" of death, through and on account of Jesus' death.
>
> The "grand gallery" measures 1874 inches long at the top, 1878 inches long at a groove cut in its sides about midway between bottom and top and 1881 inches, at the bottom. (The upper end wall impends or slants forward).
>
> Now notice how aptly these three distinct dates (1874, 1878, 1881,) are marked by the pyramid . . .
>
> Two other ways, in which the Pyramid corroborates scripture are these: At the top of the "grand gallery"—just where it measures 1874 inches, there is an opening or passage-way which seems to say, something might go out or come in here. For some time we thought this might represent the "change," or catching away of the church as spiritual beings; but it would have been due in 1874 and no translation took place; then it must mean something else. It seems plain and clear to us now that that opening can mean nothing else than what the Prophets have taught us, viz: that there the Bridegroom came a spiritual being. . . .
>
> Secondly, we are claiming that our Lord's presence here, is to be to many in the nominal church "a stone of stumbling" and this too finds its illustration in the Pyramid, for at the upper end of the "Grand gallery" a huge block of stone juts out into the pathway . . .

The *Watch Tower* of June 1, 1910, under the heading "Our Visit To the Pyramid," tells how Russell with over a dozen other representatives of the Society then travelled to Egypt for the second time: (pages 179–180)

> The chief interest of the latter place centered in the Pyramid. Since we visited it eighteen years ago several of the casing stones have been found at the base of the Pyramid by the removal of the rubbish which had covered them for centuries. . . . The Brothers Edgar, of Scotland, visited the Pyramid last year to go over the measurements of its passageways . . .
>
> We went all over the structure again—not, however, with the view of taking measurements, for these, we believe, have already been taken more accurately than instruments then at our command would permit. We merely reviewed this Great Witness to the Lord of hosts and recalled to mind its testimony, which we have already presented . . . in the last chapter of the third volume of STUDIES IN THE SCRIPTURES. . . .

This book, *Studies in the Scriptures,* Volume III, published by the Society in 1891, features numerous diagrams of Pyramid chambers and passageways, along with calculations based on their measurements. The tenth chapter, titled "THE TESTIMONY OF GOD'S STONE WITNESS AND PROPHET, THE GREAT PYRAMID IN EGYPT" (page 313, 1903 ed.) says:

> . . . the Great Pyramid . . . seems in a remarkable manner to teach, in harmony with all the prophets, an outline of the plan of God, past, present and future. . . . [page 314]
>
> The Great Pyramid, however, proves to be a storehouse of important truth—scientific, historic and prophetic—and its testimony is found to be in perfect accord with the Bible, expressing the prominent features of its truths in beautiful and fitting symbols. [pages 314–315]

It is conjectured that Melchizedek, though not himself an Egyptian, used Egyptian labor for the construction of the Great Pyramid. And to some extent the traditions of Egypt support such a theory. [page 322]

Then measuring down the "Entrance Passage" from that point, to find the distance to the entrance of the "Pit," representing the great trouble and destruction with which this age is to close, when evil will be overthrown from power, we find it to be 3416 inches, symbolizing 3416 years from the above date, B.C. 1542. This calculation shows A.D. 1874 as marking the beginning of the period of trouble; for 1542 years B.C. plus 1874 years A.D. equals 3416 years. Thus the Pyramid witnesses that the close of 1874 was the chronological beginning of the time of trouble such as was not since there was a nation—no, nor ever shall be afterward. [page 342]

Years after Russell's death, and well into the 1920s, the Watchtower Society continued to teach that Jehovah God designed the Pyramid:

In the passages of the Great Pyramid of Gizeh the agreement of one or two measurements with the present-truth chronology might be accidental, but the correspondency of dozens of measurements proves that the same God designed both pyramid and plan . . .
—*The Watch Tower,* June 15, 1922,
page 187

The great Pyramid of Egypt, standing as a silent and inanimate witness of the Lord, is a messenger; and its testimony speaks with great eloquence concerning the divine plan.
—*The Watch Tower,* May 15, 1925,
page 148

In the November 15, 1928, issue of *The Watch Tower,* however, Judge Rutherford reversed the teaching on the Pyramid, now calling it "Satan's Bible" and declaring that persons following pyramid teachings were "not following after Christ":

> If the pyramid is not mentioned in the Bible, then following its teachings is being led by vain philosophy and false science and not following after Christ. [page 341]

> It is more reasonable to conclude that the great pyramid of Gizeh, as well as the other pyramids thereabout, also the sphinx, were built by the rulers of Egypt and under the direction of Satan the Devil. . . . Then Satan put his knowledge in dead stone, which may be called Satan's Bible, and not God's stone witness. . . .

> Those who have devoted themselves to the pyramid have failed to see some of the most important things that God has revealed for the benefit of his church. The mind of such was turned away from Jehovah and his Word. [page 344]

So, then, does this mean that the Watchtower organization was "not following after Christ" during the nearly fifty years of pyramid teaching, from when C. T. Russell started publishing until this reversal in 1928? And does it mean that material published in the pages of *The Watch Tower* and the Society's books is admitted to have been taken from "Satan's Bible" and written by people whose minds were "turned away from Jehovah and his Word"? Rutherford's purpose in publishing such a denunciation of pyramidology in 1928 was, no doubt, to undermine his opponents who were still promoting loyalty to the late Pastor Russell and studying his writings in preference to books published by the Watchtower Society under its new president. But the harsh words Rutherford aimed and fired at his contemporaries have outlived both him and them, to be cited today by the Society's critics as an unwitting confession to cultic error.

Jehovah's Witnesses today are left largely in ignorance of the entire matter. Thus, a May 15, 1956, *Watchtower* article devotes four pages (297–300) to the Great Pyramid and mentions that "others" claimed it was built under divine inspiration "as a witness in stone to corroborate the Bible," naming "John Taylor of London, Professor Smyth and Dr. Edgar of Scotland" as advocates of the theory that pyramid measurements held biblical significance. A small print footnote to this discussion on page 298 adds that "Bible Students also held to this thought prior to 1928," but Pastor Russell's name is not mentioned in the article, nor the fact that Watchtower publications promoted Professor Smyth's theories and Watchtower offices distributed Dr. Edgar's books.[6] Silence on the subject in recent years has resulted in outside students of the movement generally knowing more about the role pyramidology played in its history than members themselves, but the 7-foot tall Watch Tower Pyramid north of Pittsburgh stands as a permanent reminder of this episode in the history of Jehovah's Witnesses, just as the Great Pyramid of Egypt testifies to the religion of that ancient land.

The organization's self-published history book *Jehovah's Witnesses—Proclaimers of God's Kingdom* admits on page 201, "For some 35 years Pastor Russell thought that the Great Pyramid of Gizeh was God's stone witness, corroborating Biblical time periods." However, the *Proclaimers* book fails to admit that the Society continued promoting pyramid teachings years after Russell's death in 1916, well into the presidency of Russell's successor Joseph F. ("Judge") Rutherford. For example, the May 15, 1925 *Watch Tower*, on page 148, calls the "great Pyramid of Egypt . . . a silent and inanimate witness of the Lord." In fact, it was not until the 1928 article quoted above that the Society finally ended nearly 50 years of pyramid teachings, which it then admitted had turned people away from God so that they were "not following after Christ."

The Watchtower's involvement with the pyramid may be profitably discussed with Jehovah's Witnesses by any Christian willing to put forth a bit of effort to furnish suitable documentation. Three approaches can be taken, either separately or together.

One approach would be to get the JW to read some of the material the Watchtower Society actually published on the subject. If the Witness has access to the Society's early *Studies in the Scriptures* series (originally titled *Millennial Dawn*), ask him or her to open volume 3 and read the chapter titled "The Testimony of God's Stone Witness and Prophet, the Great Pyramid in Egypt." Or, if that volume is not available, show the JW the photostats of original Watchtower material on the pyramid reproduced in my book *How to Rescue Your Loved One from the Watchtower.* Few JWs can read what the organization taught about the pyramid without finding their faith in the organization severely shaken.

Another approach would be to contrast the two viewpoints the Watchtower Society has held concerning the Great Pyramid: first, that it was "God's Stone Witness and Prophet" and, later, that it was "Satan's Bible." (*The Watch Tower*, November 15, 1928, page 344) Ask the JW whether he can safely put his trust in an organization that confuses Satan's works with God's.

A third approach focuses on the cover-up. Why does the Society's history book *Jehovah's Witnesses—Proclaimers of God's Kingdom,* a huge volume of some 750 pages, reduce 50 years of pyramid teaching to a single sentence, and a misleading one at that? If the Witness doubts that a cover-up exists, encourage him to speak to the elders at his Kingdom Hall about researching the matter. Their reaction when he tries to pull this mummified skeleton out of the closet should be enough to convince him that the organization has something to hide.

See New Light.

Race

Jehovah's Witnesses pride themselves on being free from the racial hatreds that prevail in so many lands. They like to point to their brotherly love as evidence that they belong to the one true religion. However, their claim to superiority over other churches in this regard is seriously flawed.

First of all, it may be observed that there are relatively few non-whites in the higher ranks of the Watchtower Society's organizational hierarchy. As for the topmost position, since the time of the organization's founding only white men of northern European stock Russell, Rutherford, Knorr, Franz, and Henschel—have been appointed president. The family names of the eleven Governing Body members as of this writing betray a similar narrow focus: Booth, Klein, Barber, Swingle, Schroeder, Barr, Barry, Sydlik, Henschel, Jaracz, and Lösch. Two are Slavic (Sydlik and Jaracz), but the rest are evidently Anglo-Saxon or Germanic. (Individual portrait photos of the men on the Governing Body as of January 1992 appear on page 116 of the book *Jehovah's Witnesses—Proclaimers of God's Kingdom*.) The organization draws millions to its Kingdom Halls in Africa and millions in Latin America, but as of this writing continues to exclude blacks and Hispanics from top leadership positions. True, with Governing Body members appointed to life terms turnover is slow, but the appointment of newest member Gerrit Lösch in July 1994 merely reinforces the long-standing English-Germanic monopoly, as he is Austrian by birth.

Officially, the organization today teaches racial equality. Yet one can only wonder to what extent the elderly gentlemen on the Governing Body may still be influenced by former Watchtower teaching such as this:

> . . . it is true that the white race exhibits some qualities of superiority over any other . . . The secret of the greater

intelligence and aptitude of the Caucasian undoubtedly in great measure is to be attributed to the commingling of blood amongst its various branches; and this was evidently forced in large measure by circumstances under divine control.

—*Watch Tower,* July 15, 1902, page 216, from Society's reprints, page 3043

It is true that rank-and-file Jehovah's Witnesses in mixed-race congregations today have generally come a long way toward eliminating the racial prejudice that characterized their predecessors. However, to some extent that former racism has simply been replaced by what could be called *religionism,* with JWs exhibiting prejudice against non-Witnesses in the same way that individuals of one race sometimes look down on another.

Resurrection

Christians see the empty tomb of Jesus Christ as one of the most powerful pictorial statements ever made. Its meaning is clear and simple. The angel stationed at the tomb put it into words, thus: "He is not here; he has risen, just as he said. Come and see the place where he lay." (Matthew 28:6 NIV) The Watchtower Society, however, attaches an altogether different meaning to the empty tomb, namely that God "disposed of" Jesus' body:

"God disposed of Jesus' body, not allowing it to see corruption and thus preventing its becoming a stumbling block to faith."

—*The Watchtower,* November 15, 1991, page 31

"We deny that He was raised in the flesh, and challenge any statement to that effect as being unscriptural."

—*Studies in the Scriptures,* Vol. 7, page 57

Some years ago *The Watchtower* explained in more detail what supposedly happened to the Savior's body, claiming that it "was disposed of by Jehovah God, dissolved into its constituent elements or atoms." (September 1, 1953, page 518)

What then was the real meaning of the empty tomb: that Christ's body had been resurrected or disposed of? Jesus himself is the one best qualified to answer that question, of course, and he declared ahead of time exactly what would happen to his body. He said, "I will raise it again in three days." (John 2:19) Certain Jews listening at the time thought he was talking about the stone temple building in Jerusalem when he said, "Destroy this temple, and I will raise it again in three days," but the Bible explains that "the temple he had spoken of was his body." (John 2:19–21 NIV) So, Jesus did not say his body would be "disposed of." No! He said, "I will raise it up." (John 2:19 RSV) Even the Watchtower Society's own *New World Translation* at John 2:19 has Jesus saying, "I will raise it up."

Why, though, do Jehovah's Witnesses make an issue over this matter in the first place? Why do they deny the resurrection of Christ's body? Primarily because the facts related in Scripture contradict Watchtower teachings on heaven, hell, and the afterlife in general. While Christians understand that Jesus' spirit remained alive in the invisible realm during the time his body lay in the tomb, so that *he* could raise it up on the third day, Jehovah's Witnesses are told that the body in the tomb was all that remained after Christ's death since there is no such thing as an immortal soul. His personality was annihilated at death, and then his body was "disposed of" shortly thereafter, meaning that Jesus passed out of existence completely and went into nothingness. Between the time of his death and subsequent resurrection, Jesus Christ ceased to exist, according to the sect. Then, on the third day, God created him once again as Michael the Archangel, a spirit creature without a body of flesh. (*See* Michael the Archangel.)

This same pattern is followed, JWs believe, in regard to mankind in general: we become nonexistent at death, and our future "resurrection" means that God will create us once again out of nothingness. This doctrine is proved wrong by the fact that it was Christ's body that was raised up on the third day, and that Jesus himself performed this deed—"I will raise it up"—since this points to Christ's being alive in the spirit realm in the interim, and hence to our being in line for some sort of conscious existence after death. Honesty forces us to admit here too that "what we will be has not yet been made known." (1 John 3:2 NIV) But the Bible assures us that when Christ appears "we shall be like him." (1 John 3:2) The Apostle Paul expected at death "to depart and be with Christ." (Philippians 1:23 NIV) This appears to be different from the resurrection which does not take place until "the coming of the Lord" when "the dead in Christ will rise first." (1 Thessalonians 4:15–17 NIV) A similar sequence of events seems to be assumed in the parable of the rich man and Lazarus. When Lazarus dies he is taken immediately to the place where Abraham is. Although he is conscious there, he has not been resurrected. His resurrection is presented as a future event as the characters in the parable discuss the possibility of sending him to warn the rich man's living brothers. They discuss whether the brothers would be convinced "even if someone rises from the dead"—*i.e.*, is resurrected. (Luke 16:31 NIV)

Determined to deny what Scripture plainly states, the Watchtower Society has long claimed that "the man Jesus is dead, forever dead" (*Studies in the Scriptures,* Vol. 5, page 454) even though the Bible speaks of our living mediator as "a man, Christ Jesus." (1 Timothy 2:5 NWT) The Society's reasoning is as follows: "Having given up his flesh for the life of the world, Christ could never take it again and become a man once more." (*You Can Live Forever in Paradise on Earth*, page 143) Resurrecting Christ's body would be impossible, JWs quickly add, since that would constitute taking back the ransom price he paid for our sins. However, Jesus himself proved that argument wrong when he said, "I lay down my life for the sheep . . . I lay down my life—only to take it up again. . . . I have authority to lay it down and authority to take it up again." (John 10:14–18 NIV) Taking it up again did not in any way invalidate the fact that he had laid down his life in sacrifice for us.

Interestingly, the Watchtower Society's claim that "Jehovah saw fit to remove Jesus' body" (*You Can Live Forever in Paradise on Earth*, page 144) echoes the charge made by first century Jewish leaders. They approached Pontius Pilate with this thought:

> "Sir," they said, "we remember that while he was still alive that deceiver said, 'After three days I will rise again.' So give the order for the tomb to be made secure until the third day. Otherwise, his disciples may come and steal the body and tell the people that he has been raised from the dead. This last deception will be worse than the first." (Matthew 27:63–64 NIV)

However, it was not the mere absence of his body from the tomb that proved Jesus was alive; it was the fact that he was up and about, walking around and showing himself to his followers. He said to them, "Look at my hands and my feet. It is I myself! Touch me and see; a ghost does not have flesh and bones, as you see I have." (Luke 24:39 NIV)

The resurrected Christ was no angelic spirit creature named Michael according to these words of Scripture. Even the JW *New World Translation* has him saying, "See my hands and my feet, that it is I myself; feel me and see, because a spirit does not have flesh and bones just as you behold that I have." (Luke 24:39 NWT) This was the same

Christ who died on the cross, complete with nail holes in his hands and feet:

> Now Thomas (called Didymus), one of the Twelve, was not with the disciples when Jesus came. So the other disciples told him, "We have seen the Lord!" But he said to them, "Unless I see the nail marks in his hands and put my finger where the nails were, and put my hand into his side, I will not believe it." A week later his disciples were in the house again, and Thomas was with them. Though the doors were locked, Jesus came and stood among them and said, "Peace be with you!" Then he said to Thomas, "Put your finger here; see my hands. Reach out your hand and put it into my side. Stop doubting and believe." (John 20:24–27 NIV)

Instead of accepting this evidence that brought doubting Thomas to his knees, the Watchtower book *You Can Live Forever in Paradise on Earth* explains that Jesus tricked the apostle Thomas into thinking his disposed-of body had actually been resurrected: "In order to convince Thomas of who He was, He used a body with wound holes." (page 145)

Unwilling to accept the testimony of Scripture, Jehovah's Witnesses find themselves "forever changing our minds about what we believe because someone has told us something different, or has cleverly lied to us and made the lie sound like the truth" (Ephesians 4:14 *The Living Bible*'s paraphrase)—especially in the matter of the resurrection. For example, the organization taught in 1879 that the men of ancient Sodom will be resurrected, in 1952 that they will not, in 1965 that they will indeed be resurrected after all, and in 1988 that they actually will not be resurrected. (*The Watchtower*, July 1879, page 8; June 1, 1952, page 338; August 1, 1965, page 479; and June 1, 1988, page 31)

How preferable it is, rather than follow the storm-tossed teachings of men, to be like the first-century believers in accepting the empty tomb as proof that Christ is risen and that we can "be united with him in his resurrection." (Romans 6:5 NIV)

See Heaven, Hell, *and* Soul & Spirit.

Russell

Publication of the first *Watch Tower* magazine in July 1879 marks the birth of Russellism and of the sect that later took on the name Jehovah's Witnesses. True, Charles Taze Russell had earlier written a pamphlet titled *The Object and Manner of The Lord's Return,* and his name appeared under N. H. Barbour's on the title page of the book *The Three Worlds,* but these publications and the articles he wrote for Barbour's *Herald of the Morning* magazine were all produced while Russell remained under the tutelage of his Adventist mentors. (*See* Adventist Origins.) It was with the first issue of *Zion's Watch Tower* that he emerged as an independent religious leader.

Yet even then, the formation of a distinct denomination around Charles Taze Russell was a gradual development. At first the *Watch Tower* was mailed to the Adventist readers of the *Herald of the Morning,* Russell having taken with him a copy of that magazine's mailing list when he resigned as assistant editor. The two journals, in agreement on most major matters, warred against each other over per sonalities and other minor matters, battling for the minds of their joint readership. Russell's immediate break was not with Adventism, but with the person and policies of N. H. Barbour.

Nor were barriers immediately erected with respect to Protestantism in general. New readers obtaining subscriptions to *Zion's Watch Tower* were often church members who saw the magazine as a para-church ministry rather than an anti-church alternative. Russell traveled about speaking from the pulpits of Protestant churches as well as to gatherings of his own followers. In 1879, the year he married Maria Frances Ackley and also the year he began publishing *Zion's Watch Tower,* Russell organized some thirty study groups or congregations scattered from Ohio to the New England coast. Each local "class" or *ecclesia* recognized him as "Pastor," although geography and Russell's writing and publishing activities prevented more than an occasional pastoral visit in person. During 1883 the possibility of forming a new denomination was discussed more than once in the pages of his periodical, but each time his editorial position was that "a visible organization, and the adopting of some particular name" should be rejected as appealing only to the worldly, natural man, while believers should be content to belong only to Christ's "perfect organization, invisible to the world." (*Zion's Watch Tower,* March, 1883, page 458 Society's reprints) He maintained that through his publishing and public speaking campaigns "no earthly organization is attempted" or needed since "we are as one—all united to the one head and following the leadings of his Word and Spirit." (*Zion's Watch Tower,* October, 1883, page 536 Society's reprints)

In time, though, Russell's increasingly divergent teachings forced his followers to separate from other church bodies and to create one of their own. Beginning as he did in a small branch of Adventism that held to a conditionalist version of redemption and that carried dispensationalism to the extreme of setting specific dates for the return of Christ and the Rapture, Russell went farther out on a limb in 1882 by openly rejecting the doctrine of the Trinity. His earlier mentor Nelson H. Barbour was a trinitarian, as was the *Herald of the Morning*'s other assistant editor John H. Paton, who joined Russell in leaving to start *Zion's Watch Tower.* The writings of Barbour and Paton that Russell had helped publish or distribute were trinitarian in their theology. And the *Watch Tower* itself was at first vague and noncommittal on the subject. It was only after

Paton broke with him and ceased to be listed on the masthead that Russell wrote

> Our readers are aware that while we believe in Jehovah and Jesus and the holy spirit, we reject as totally unscriptural, the teaching that these are three Gods in one person, or as some put it, one God in three persons. The doctrine of the Trinity had its rise in the third century, and has a close resemblance to the heathen doctrines prevalent at that time, particularly Hindooism.
>
> —*Zion's Watch Tower*, July, 1882, page 369 Society's reprints

Another aspect of Russell's teachings that helped separate him and his followers from the more traditional churches was his focus on the pyramids of Egypt, in particular the Great Pyramid of Giza. He personally led an entourage of followers on a pilgrimage to the ancient burial ground of the Pharaohs on more than one occasion, and he wrote at length to prove a prophetic connection between internal pyramid measurements and the timing of world events. The dates he set for the Rapture and the end of the world derived, in part, from pyramid measurements. (*See* Pyramid.)

Much has been written on the subject of Russell's divorce or separation from his wife. The recent Watchtower publication *Jehovah's Witnesses—Proclaimers of God's Kingdom* provides this information:

> In 1879, Charles Taze Russell married Maria Frances Ackley . . . in November 1897 she left him . . . she was awarded, in 1908, a judgment, not of absolute divorce, but of divorce from bed and board, with alimony.
>
> —page 645

While some opposers of the Watchtower organization may be too quick to believe every charge made against the

Society's first president, JWs have, no doubt, been too quick to lay the blame for their divorce entirely at his wife's feet. After sifting out the more emotional and exaggerated charges and counter-charges, it would still seem that there was enough blame to go around, with both parties sharing responsibility for the marriage failure. So, it would be a valid question to ask, in view of his conduct toward his wife, whether C. T. Russell would qualify as a JW elder or as a pastor of a Bible-believing church.

Looking back at Russell's presidency and the years immediately following his death, the Watchtower Society makes this amazing admission:

> In the early part of our 20th century prior to 1919, the Bible Students, as Jehovah's Witnesses were then known, had to be released from a form of spiritual captivity to the ideas and practices of false religion . . . Some were exalting creatures, indulging in a personality cult that focused on Charles T. Russell, the first president of the Watch Tower Bible and Tract Society.
>
> —May 1, 1989, *Watchtower*, page 4

The Society blames this "cult" on "some" within its ranks. But who actually promoted the cult? The evidence points to Russell himself and those associated with him in running the Society. After all, a few "apostates" in their midst could hardly have been responsible for statements in the Society's publications exalting Russell over a period of many years. For example, the November 1, 1917, *Watch Tower*, carried an article titled "A Tribute to the Seventh Messenger" in which it said (Society's reprints, page 6159):

> The two most prominent messengers, however, are the first and the last—St. Paul and Pastor Russell. . . . "That wise and faithful servant" . . . now many more are recognizing, that Pastor Russell is that servant.

By the time of his death on October 31, 1916, Charles Taze Russell had traveled more than a million miles and preached more than 30,000 sermons. He had authored works totalling some 50,000 printed pages, and nearly 20,000,000 copies of his books and booklets had been sold. (*Jehovah's Witnesses in the Divine Purpose*, page 62; and *The Laodicean Messenger*, page 106)

Russell's followers split up after his death to form several sects, including the one that Joseph Rutherford renamed Jehovah's Witnesses in 1931 to distinguish it from the other Bible Students groups.

See Adventist Origins.

Rutherford

When Charles Taze Russell died thirty-seven years after commencing publication of *Zion's Watch Tower* magazine, a bitter factional battle rocked the organization he left behind. Although Russell had prepared detailed written instructions distributing his authority among several of his followers, second President Joseph F. Rutherford ignored his predecessor's will and sought instead to consolidate power in his own hands. Having served as legal counsel for Russell and the Society, attorney Rutherford was in a unique position to use corporate law to wage "spiritual" warfare. (His widely recognized nickname "Judge" Rutherford derives from a brief interim of service on the bench as a substitute jurist.)

The book *Faith on the March* by A. H. Macmillan, privately published in 1957 with Watchtower approval and still found in many Kingdom Hall libraries, gives some details of this battle from the viewpoint of the winning faction—with the aim of discrediting the losers. Viewed objectively, however, the account actually discredits the entire organization. Among other things, Macmillan reveals that the pro-Rutherford minority on the Society's Board of

Directors had the police brought in to expel the anti-Rutherford majority from the Society's offices. (pages 79, 80) Rutherford then proceeded to use a legal loophole to replace the Directors appointed by Russell, installing his own supporters in their place. According to the sect's official history book *Jehovah's Witnesses—Proclaimers of God's Kingdom*, "Four members of the board of directors of the Society went so far as to endeavor to wrest administrative control from Rutherford's hands." (pages 66–68) Since page 65 mentions in a footnote that there were a total of seven on the board of directors, the four opposed to Rutherford therefore constituted the majority of the Governing Body. Had they managed to outwit Rutherford legally, the Society's official history would no doubt have portrayed him as the renegade.

After securing complete control over the headquarters offices and the sect's corporate entities, "the Judge" undertook a gradual but deliberate effort to eliminate democratic church government in the local congregations of "Bible Students" around the globe. First he appointed a Service Director in each congregation to handle the literature shipped in from Brooklyn; then he began increasing the responsibilities of his appointees and decreasing the authority of locally elected elders. His aim was an organization ruled from the top down. It was not autocratic, however, because Rutherford was not in charge; he took his commands from God, so it was a "theocratic" organization. He even banned youth groups and Sunday school classes for children during the 1930s because they did "not contribute to unity." (*Jehovah's Witnesses—Proclaimers of God's Kingdom*, pages 246–247) All meeting attenders, young and old alike, were to receive the same indoctrination.

The first book published under Rutherford's presidency proclaimed that the dead Pastor Russell was still running the organization from "beyond the veil." (*The Finished Mystery*, 1917, pages 144, 256) However, as the second president consolidated his control, he also began changing Russell's doctrines to suit his own taste. For example, Russell had taught that the Great Pyramid of Egypt was inspired by Jehovah God, and he used Pyramid measurements in both chronology and prophecy. Rutherford maintained this teaching for over a decade, but then reversed the Society's position and credited the Pyramid to Satan the Devil instead of God. (*See* Pyramid.) Under Russell the Watchtower organization acknowledged that Jesus was not born on December 25th, but encouraged followers not to "quibble" about the date but rather to join "in celebrating the grand event on the day which the majority celebrate—Christmas day.'" (*Watch Tower,* December 1, 1904, page 3468 Society's reprints) Judge Rutherford later decided to quibble—as part of an overall process of de-emphasizing Christ. (*See* Christmas.) Rutherford's new teachings on the Great Crowd and the Other Sheep effectively closed the door to the heavenly hope in 1935 and divided Jehovah's Witnesses into two classes: a dwindling elite of heaven-bound leaders and a growing throng of earthly subjects.

Though his lectures attacked "Big Business" and the wealthy class with the fervor of a populist politician, "the Judge" freely indulged himself with the organization's growing resources. He drove sixteen-cylinder cars, had the Beth-Sarim mansion built in San Diego, and lived there with a staff of servants. A heavy drinker, he denounced Prohibition and had high Watchtower officials smuggling liquor into Brooklyn from Toronto, according to Canadian historian M. James Penton. (*Apocalypse Delayed: The Story of Jehovah's Witnesses,* University of Toronto Press, 1985, page 225)

Rutherford had a wife Mary who resided apart from him in another state "where the climate was better for her health." (*Jehovah's Witnesses—Proclaimers of God's Kingdom,* page 85) They fathered a son, Malcolm, before splitting up, and there was no public divorce proceeding as there was in Russell's case. Still, the estrangement during their later years adds to the impression that Watchtower leaders have typically had difficulty in their relationship with women. (*See* Marriage.)

Under Rutherford's presidency from 1917 to 1941 the organization produced 24 books and 86 booklets in addition to a constant flood of periodicals. None of these remain in use among Jehovah's Witnesses today. In fact, they are filled with abandoned interpretations, discontinued doctrines, and failed prophecies. (*See* False Prophecies.) In a moment of unusual candor *The Watchtower* of October 1, 1984, features an autobiographical article by Governing Body member Karl Klein in which he observes how Rutherford felt about his prophetic failures: "Regarding his misguided statements as to what we could expect in 1925, he once confessed to us at Bethel, 'I made an ass of myself.'" (page 24)

Salvation

There are a number of problems with the Jehovah's Witness view of salvation: it is elusive, works-oriented, and different for two classes of believers. The JW is trained to look to the organization for salvation rather than look to Christ. "To get one's name written in that Book of Life will depend upon one's works" (*The Watchtower*, April 1, 1947, page 204), they are told, so Witnesses find themselves "working hard for the reward of eternal life." (*The Watchtower*, August 15, 1972, page 491)

During my eight years as an elder, fellow Jehovah's Witnesses occasionally confided in me, expressing doubts and fears that troubled them deep inside. I was surprised, though, when our friend "Myrtle" (not her real name) told me what was bothering her. She had served the Watchtower for decades and was then, in her seventies, still going strong—preaching door-to-door full time, although not with the same strength she had displayed in her younger days when she was able to work a full-time job and raise a family, besides going out from house to house. One day as we were working together in the door-to-door ministry, Myrtle paused between houses and turned to me.

"David," she said, "I know I'm not going to make it through Armageddon—I'm not good enough!"

Needless to say, I was shocked. "But, Myrtle," I tried to reason with her, "you've accomplished more than most of us at Kingdom Hall. If you won't make it into the New Order, how could any of us hope to survive?"

"I don't know about that," she answered, shaking her head, "but I know that Jehovah isn't pleased with me. I'm not good enough. I'm not going to be there in the Paradise."

I was shocked then, but now I realize that Jehovah's Witnesses fall into one of two categories: (1) those who self-righteously assume that God will preserve them through Armageddon on account of their good works, and (2) those who know they are sinners unworthy of eternal life. I myself fell into the first category; Myrtle fell into the second.

Since then, I have learned that I was wrong and Myrtle was right. Independent Bible reading eventually led me to Romans, chapter 8, which says that "those who are in the flesh cannot please God." (verse 8 RSV)

Myrtle felt that she could not please God no matter how hard she tried, and she was right because, "those who are in the flesh cannot please God." The only ones not in the flesh, and therefore able to please God, are those who have received the Spirit "of sonship" (verse 15) as "fellow heirs with Christ" who would eventually be "glorified" with Him. (verse 17)

But the Watchtower had taught us that there are only 144,000 individuals down through the centuries who receive God's Spirit to become joint heirs with Christ, who will end up glorified with Him in heaven—that only a small remnant of a few thousand such spirit-anointed individuals remain alive on earth, whereas the millions of average Jehovah's Witnesses do not receive the Spirit as discussed at Romans, chapter 8.

No wonder, then, that so many JWs—like Myrtle—feel guilty, condemned, and unable to please God! The Scriptures make it plain:

> those who are in the flesh cannot please God. But you are not in the flesh, you are in the Spirit, if in fact the Spirit of God dwells in you. Any one who does not have the Spirit of Christ does not belong to him.
> . . . but you have received the spirit of sonship. When we cry, "Abba! Father!" it is the Spirit himself bearing witness with our spirit that we are children of God, and if children, then heirs, heirs of God and fellow heirs with Christ . . .
> —Romans 8:8–9, 15–17 RSV

The Watchtower Society consigns its "great crowd" of non-spirit-anointed followers to a position where they "cannot please God" no matter how hard they try.

The doubts and fears that plague Jehovah's Witnesses like Myrtle have a common solution: the individual must put his or her trust in Jesus Christ rather than in the Watchtower. Whereas Myrtle felt condemned while serving in the Watchtower organization, "There is therefore now no condemnation for those who are in Christ Jesus." (Romans 8:1 RSV) Whereas many of my JW friends felt bitterly disappointed as they faced death in their old age,

> the law of the Spirit of life in Christ has set me free from the law of sin and death . . .
> . . . if Christ is in you, although your bodies are dead because of sin, your spirits are alive because of righteousness. If the Spirit of him who raised Jesus from the dead

dwells in you, he who raised Christ Jesus from the dead will give life to your mortal bodies also through his Spirit which dwells in you.

—Romans 8:2, 10–12 RSV

Instead of trusting in *The Watchtower*'s invitation to "come to Jehovah's organization for salvation" (November 15, 1981, page 21), Jehovah's Witnesses need to respond to Jesus Christ who says, "Come to me, all of you who are tired from carrying heavy loads, and I will give you rest." Also, "I will never turn away anyone who comes to me." (Matthew 11:28–29; John 6:37 *Today's English Version*)

See also Heaven *and* Justification.

Shunning

In November of 1988, nine million people suddenly changed their minds. They all decided to start talking to certain family members and acquaintances they had previously been avoiding. Why did they all change their minds unanimously and simultaneously? Because they read the November 15, 1988, issue of *The Watchtower*, and it told them to do so.

This was not the first time *The Watchtower* had issued new instructions on the matter of shunning. For some read ers there was a relative they had stopped talking to in the early 1970s, started talking to again in 1974, and then stopped talking to once more in 1981. Now they were talking to that same person again in 1988—not because the person kept changing, but because the Watchtower Society kept changing its instructions.

Those instructions are rather complex as they differentiate among various categories of shunned individuals and as they spell out the forms of contact that are or are not permissible in various circumstances. The elders form a "judicial committee" and "disfellowship" (expel) members who commit sexual immorality or who express dis- agreement with the Watchtower Society on any issue. The individual expelled for apostate thinking is shunned more completely than the JW disfellowshiped for fornication or adultery. One who voluntarily leaves the sect faces the same penalty at the hands of a judicial committee, but is considered "disassociated" rather than "disfellowshiped." Much like the diplomatic protocol that governs hand- shakes at formal meetings between ambassadors and heads of state, organizational instructions tell Witnesses how to behave in the case of shunned friends and shunned relatives, relatives inside and outside the immediate fam- ily, those living in the home and those not living in the home, and so on. JWs must keep abreast with the latest changes in such instructions, because failure to observe the current protocol results in their being taken to task by the elders.

Visitors at Kingdom Hall meetings seldom learn about shunning right away or learn of the closed-door interro- gations and trials held constantly to keep members in line. With press and media relations handled only by assigned spokesmen—always men, never women—trained in the art of euphemism, the sect usually manages to keep the internal disciplinary system hidden from the public eye, and hence to maintain a fairly good public image.

The other side of the story is usually told in detail only by persons who have lived part of their lives in the group and, after leaving, have somehow been able to escape the fear and guilt that keep most former members quiet. When ex-JWs do speak out, the story that emerges is reminiscent of life in Nicolae Ceausescu's Romania where the Security Police were everywhere spying on people's private lives and forcing children to testify against their own parents. Many former Witnesses compare the Watchtower king- dom to the futuristic dictatorship of George Orwell's novel *Nineteen Eighty-Four* where "Big Brother is watching you!"

As mentioned at the beginning of this discussion, for many families of Jehovah's Witnesses the Watchtower Society's back-and-forth changes in policy on shunning have produced an up-and-down sort of existence such as one might experience at the end of a yo-yo string. First, they could speak to certain relatives; then, they could not; then, they could speak again; once more, they could not; and so on. More than any of the Watchtower's other doctrinal changes, these reversals in regard to who must be shunned have wreaked havoc in the lives and emotions of affected individuals and their families.

In 1972, for example, the new book *Organization for Kingdom Preaching and Disciple Making* retained and reinforced the strict shunning policies of the earlier book, *Your Word Is A Lamp to My Foot*, which had been used during the 1960s as a handbook for organizational matters. Witnesses knew that they could not say so much as *hello* to someone who had been expelled, and that they were obligated to keep away from relatives who were disfellowshiped. Then, in 1974, the August 1st *Watchtower* featured a lengthy discussion modifying and softening those policies:

> Thus, Jesus' own example protects us against adopting the extreme view of certain rabbinical writers in this matter of dealing with persons as "a man of the nations and as a tax collector." . . . as Jesus' example shows, this does not require our treating such a one as an enemy or refusing to show common courtesy and consideration. . . . There is . . . nothing to show that Jews with a balanced and Scriptural viewpoint would refuse to greet a "man of the nations" or a tax collector. Jesus' counsel about greetings, in connection with his exhortation to imitate God in his undeserved kindness toward "wicked people and good," would seem to rule against such a rigid stand. . . . when sons or daughters render honor to a parent, though disfellowshiped, by calling to see how such a one's physical health is or what needs

213

he or she may have, this act in itself is not a spiritual fellowshiping.

—pages 464–465, 471

This "balanced and Scriptural viewpoint" prevailed until 1981, when the Society reversed itself again and returned to the more severe treatment that had been required before 1974, announcing this in the September 15, 1981, *Watchtower*. Witnesses then had to stop greeting those they had been greeting from '74 to '81 and stop honoring the parents they had been honoring during those years. Since 1981, the more extreme form of shunning has been required. In its November 15, 1988, issue, however, *The Watchtower* once more reversed the policy insofar as it applies to unbaptized persons, including children raised in the organization: "Previously, unbaptized ones who unrepentantly sinned were completely avoided," but now the magazine makes a technical distinction regarding a youngster raised in the sect but not baptized: "The Bible does not require that Witnesses avoid speaking with him, for he is not disfellowshipped." (page 19)

On a personal note, these changes in the Watchtower Society's shunning policy served as a painful reminder of what had happened in my own family. When I was baptized as a Jehovah's Witness in 1969, I was already conducting studies with my mother and my sister Barbara. They both smoked, but that was permissible at the time. There were many other JWs who smoked, and smokers could be baptized. Well, soon after they both took this step, the Society changed the rules and announced that smokers would no longer be accepted for baptism, and that baptized Witnesses who smoked had six months to quit, or they would be disfellowshiped.

When they failed to quit within the allotted time, my mother and my sister were expelled. The *Organization* book required me to cut them off, so I complied. Then, a couple of years later, the August 1, 1974 *Watchtower* gave us new instructions to greet disfellowshiped persons and to visit previously shunned relatives. So, I was permitted to see them again—that is, until the September 15, 1981 *Watchtower* reversed the rule once more.

This time, however, my wife and I chose not to obey. In fact, we left the organization a few months later. When Barbara died of a brain hemorrhage shortly after that, I had to preach at my own sister's funeral, because none of our long-time Witness friends would speak to us, and we had not yet made new friends outside. The only consolation for my wife and me was that we had not been shunning my mother and Barbara during the final weeks before my sister's death.

Soul & Spirit

When you die, according to Jehovah's Witnesses, you cease to exist. They deny that there is any immaterial part of man that lives on after the death of the body. In order to teach this, of course, they must redefine *soul* and *spirit*. However, that task is not as difficult as it may seem, because the Bible uses the terms in varied senses determined by context, and the English-language words *soul* and *spirit* are among those for which the dictionary lists a number of meanings. Jehovah's Witnesses take advantage of this by focusing on the definitions that can be adapted to their doctrine and ignoring those that conflict with it.

For example, there are places where the Bible uses its original language word for *soul* simply to mean a *person* ("And we were in all in the ship two hundred threescore and sixteen souls"—Acts 27:37, KJV) and other places where *soul* means *life* ("the assemblies of violent men have sought after my soul"—Psalm 86:14, KJV), so Jehovah's Witnesses cite such examples to prove that the soul is never an immaterial thing that survives the death of the body. In fact they even quote Ezekiel 18:4 out of context to prove that the soul

215

"dies." Here the King James Version does say that "the soul that sinneth, it shall die," but the context reveals that the question of whether part of man survives death is not even addressed in the passage; it deals with the charge that God punishes sons for their fathers' sins, and makes the point that the soul (or person) who sins is the one who will die. "The soul who sins is the one who will die." (NIV) (For more on this and other verses misapplied by the Witnesses, see *Jehovah's Witnesses Answered Verse by Verse*.)

In order to deny that the Bible ever uses the word *soul* to refer to a part of man that survives death, JWs carefully avoid passages that use the word in that very way, or, if confronted with such verses, they attempt to explain them away with complex arguments. Scripture passages which do clearly speak of the soul as surviving death—even in the JW *New World Translation*—include Revelation 6:9–11 ("the souls of those slaughtered . . . cried with a loud voice . . . were told to rest a little while longer . . . their brothers who were about to be killed as they also had been") and Matthew 10:28 ("do not become fearful of those who kill the body but cannot kill the soul"). The plain meaning of these texts is obvious to all but those who have been blinded by brainwashing indoctrination.

In much the same way as it denies the deity and the personality of the Holy Spirit, the Watchtower Society similarly redefines man's *spirit* as an impersonal life force: "The spirit has no personality . . . It cannot think . . . it might be likened to the electric current of a car's battery." (*The Truth That Leads to Eternal Life*, page 39) So, when Stephen asked Jesus to "receive my spirit" (Acts 7:59) he was simply asking Jesus to "pull the plug" on his life force, in the JW view.

This interpretation ignores scriptures that attribute thought and personality to man's spirit, such as 1 Corinthians 2:11 which says, "For who among men knows the thoughts of a man except the man's spirit within him?" and Mark 2:8 which says, "Jesus knew in his spirit that this was what they were thinking." (NIV) If it were a mere impersonal force like electricity, how could Jesus be "deeply moved in spirit and troubled"? (John 11:33 NIV) How could he say concerning his apostles, "The spirit is willing, but the body is weak"? (Mark 14:38 NIV) Can a force like electricity be willing?

Once you have shown a JW that the Watchtower Society is mistaken in its teachings on man's soul and spirit, the Witness may attempt to turn the tables on you by asking you to define both words and to spell out in detail a scenario of what happens at the time of death. This is a trap that should be avoided. Even if sincerely seeking answers, the sect member requires a lot of deprogramming before he or she can successfully begin relearning doctrine and theology. Or, if the JW is merely hoping that you will "cast your pearls" so that he can "turn and rip you open," it will be best to deprive him of the opportunity.

Let it suffice that you have discredited the Watchtower's misuse of the words *soul* and *spirit,* and have proved the Bible teaches survival after death. Reinforce your lesson with a reminder that Lazarus was "carried off by the angels" at death to a place where he found "comfort." (Luke 16:22, 25 NWT) Point out that Paul knew his physical death meant "being with Christ" (Philippians 1:23), "to become absent from the body and to make our home with the Lord." (2 Corinthians 5:8 NWT) Thus Jesus could truthfully say that Christians who put faith in Him "will never die at all." (John 11:26 NWT)

See also Heaven, Hell, Paradise, *and* Resurrection.

Trinity

To the Jehovah's Witness mind the Trinity is a repugnant three-headed false god invented by Satan the Devil. Belief in the Trinity ranks next to taking a blood transfusion as blatant proof of unfaithfulness to the God of the

Bible. Determined to correct this view, Christians often select the Trinity doctrine as the starting point for discussions with Jehovah's Witnesses. Just as often, however, they find that such discussions end only in frustration. Why is this the case?

First of all, JWs receive more training and get more practice arguing against this doctrine than any other. Their *Watchtower* magazine has been advancing arguments against the Trinity since 1882. They are prepared to present one Bible verse after another in apparent support of their position, and to spend hours doing this. In each instance, however, their argument can be easily refuted. (See my book *Jehovah's Witnesses Answered Verse by Verse*.) Still, the JW will not accept the Trinity.

The real problem is spiritual, rather than intellectual, and that is why reasoning and logic seem to accomplish so little: "the natural man receiveth not the things of the Spirit of God: for they are foolishness unto him: neither can he know them, because they are spiritually discerned." (1 Corinthians 2:14 KJV) When Jesus asked, "Who do you say I am?" and Peter gave the correct answer, Jesus replied, "Blessed are you, Simon son of Jonah, for this was not revealed to you by man, but by my Father in heaven." (Matthew 16:15–17 NIV) As long as a Jehovah's Witness views the Watchtower Society as God's channel of communication and trusts in his own obedience to Watchtower commands as the way to gain a righteous standing with God, it is unlikely that he will be granted the spiritual discernment needed to peer into the nature of God.

Moreover, even when a JW begins to question his beliefs and to search for God, starting him off with the Trinity doctrine is like introducing a youngster to mathematics by starting him off with college calculus instead of elementary arithmetic. In most cases it is necessary for a Witness *first* to discover that the Watchtower organization is a false prophet incapable of providing salvation, *second* to recognize a personal need for the Savior Jesus Christ, and *third* to undertake a systematic study with the aim of deprogramming and relearning. Watchtower ideas must be removed from the brain one by one and be replaced with accurate Bible understanding.

Even at that point in time it is usually best to approach theological questions with a JW (or former JW) in this sequence:

1 Demonstrate that Jesus is *not* a mere angel. (*See* Michael the Archangel.) Allow time for the Witness to get accustomed to this knowledge before pressing on to establish who Jesus is.

2 Allow Scripture to reveal the *personality* of the Holy Spirit. (*See* Holy Spirit.)

3 Let the individual read the four Gospels—maybe even the whole New Testament—in a Bible that does not contain the *New World Translation*'s theological distortions.

4 Point out biblically the deity of Christ and the deity of the Holy Spirit.

5 Explain that, although the Bible does not feature the word *Trinity*, it is a term that believers have found helpful in expressing the biblical concept that the Father is God, the Son is God, and the Holy Spirit is God, yet there is only one God.

Pushing new ex-JWs on the issue of the Trinity seldom gets them to accept it; rather, such pressure sometimes pushes them back into the Watchtower camp, or drives them to fellowship among themselves in isolated groups. The best approach, in my experience, is to lead them to God's Word and allow the Holy Spirit to teach them correct theology.

See Deity, Holy Spirit, *and* Jesus Christ.

Unity

Jehovah's Witnesses like to contrast their "speaking in agreement" (1 Corinthians 1:10) with the alleged disagreement found in "the churches." Do Jehovah's Witnesses in fact display greater agreement among themselves than members of other denominations do among themselves?

Simply answered yes or no, that can be a "loaded question"—like answering, "Have you stopped beating your wife?" or, more apropos, "Do the Chinese display greater unity than the Americans?" After the Tiananmen Square massacre the Chinese certainly do display greater unity—they don't dare disagree! But of what value is that unity if it is forced, or compelled by fear, or maintained by propagandizing the population while denying access to dissenting literature? Yet that is precisely the way the Watchtower Society maintains the unity of its followers: as in China, dissidents are removed, while the rest of the JW population is fed repetitive Watchtower material and forbidden to read other religious literature.

During the centuries of the Inquisition the Roman Catholic Church was able to instill a similar forced unity in its followers; since "heretics" were tortured and burned at the stake, hardly anyone dared to dissent.

A lesson in unity can also be learned by looking at the nations of the former Soviet bloc and the former member-states of the Soviet Union itself. Today those nations are experiencing divisions, strife, and even open warfare in some cases. But a few years ago they were able to boast of unity. They may have credited their ideology for such unity, claiming that their unity identified communism as the best form of social organization. But the facts have since shown that the unity they enjoyed in the past stemmed from mere dictatorial power, not superior ideology. When the power over them was gone, the unity also disappeared. (The Nazis, whose ideology was opposed to communism, produced similar unity among their subjects when they exercised dictatorial power.)

On occasion, the Watchtower Society has actually acknowledged that the unity within the ranks of Jehovah's Witnesses likewise stems from the organization's power over them. It quotes a loyal JW as saying,

> "I have discovered that there is only one religious organization on earth capable of clearly defining the boundaries of relative freedom. What particularly convinced me during my study with Jehovah's Witnesses is the fact that this organization has the strength to require of its members that they stay within these boundaries."
>
> —*Awake!*, March 8, 1988, page 19

The "unity" that Jehovah's Witnesses boast about is, more correctly, uniformity. All 12 million people who attend their meetings read the same material, hear the same music, sing the same songs, and learn to think the same thoughts. This rigid uniformity is not what God had in mind when He inspired the Apostles to speak and write about Christian unity. Theirs was based not on a monolithic organizational structure but on love. ". . . love, for it is a perfect bond of union." ". . . love, which binds all things together in perfect unity." (Colossians 3:14 NWT, TEV)

Does this unity based on love require the uniformity Jehovah's Witnesses display? Not according to the Apostle Paul. He showed that there is room for diversity in the Christian congregation, even in some areas of belief and practice:

> "People range from those who believe they may eat any sort of meat to those whose faith is so weak they dare not eat anything except vegetables. Meat eaters must not despise the scrupulous. On the other hand, the scrupulous must not condemn those who feel free to eat anything they choose . . . If one man keeps certain days as holier than oth-

ers, and another considers all days to be equally holy, each must be left free to hold his own opinion."

—Romans 14:2–5 *Jerusalem Bible*

By disfellowshiping Witnesses who choose to observe certain days as holy or holidays, the Watchtower goes directly against the counsel of this verse. True Christians, on the other hand, may differ with one another on issues such as diet and holidays, but still lovingly accept one another as brothers and sisters in the faith. Because they eat different foods or celebrate on different dates, they may find it necessary to meet in different groups or "denominations." Yet, if they can do this in the spirit of Romans 14 they can still be at unity with one another.

See also Church/Churches.

Vaccination

Throughout the 1930s and 1940s Watchtower publications frequently denounced vaccination as a procedure that was not only worthless but actually harmful from a medical standpoint, and morally wrong from a religious or biblical standpoint. The latter, of course, was the deciding factor for Witnesses. The organization had taught them that "Vaccination is a direct violation of the everlasting covenant that God made with Noah after the flood." (*Golden Age* [former name of *Awake!* magazine], February 4, 1931, page 293) So Jehovah's Witnesses routinely refused vaccinations for themselves and their children. If inoculation against smallpox was required for admission to public school, some Witnesses would have a sympathetic doctor burn a mark on the child's arm with acid to make it look as if the youngster had been vaccinated. Others went so far as to have papers made out falsely certifying that the child had been vaccinated.

After opposing vaccination for some twenty years Watchtower publications quietly dropped the ban in the early 1950s, and today they recommend the procedure and credit it with curbing disease. Since smallpox had been brought under control through vaccination of the non-Witness population as a whole, there was little likelihood of a JW encountering the highly contagious disease. Refusal to be vaccinated was therefore more of a nuisance problem than a life-threatening one. The value of this information today lies in its usefulness in demonstrating the man-made nature of Watchtower medical doctrines. Should a JW stake his life or his child's life on the reliability of the leadership's interpretations prohibiting blood transfusions? Let him consider first the organization's track record on vaccination.

See also Blood Transfusion *and* Organ Transplants.

Voting

"Voting costs man religion, friends—Jehovah's Witnesses 'disassociate' member." So reads the headline of a front page story in the July 16, 1993 edition of Butler, Pennsylvania's local newspaper, the *Butler Eagle*. The article tells of a 33-year-old life-long Witness who was being shunned by family and friends to punish him for voting in the 1992 primary and general elections. None of his former associates would speak to him or acknowledge him on the street following the formal "disassociation" announcement by the local elders. (*See* Shunning.)

The unusual aspect of this case was not that the individual was expelled and shunned for the "sin" of voting—such disciplinary action is virtually automatic according to regulations published internally for JW elders—but rather that a life-long Witness would take such a bold and independent step in the first place. This act of participation in democratic government is strictly forbidden to members of the sect.

Even in a country like the United States where *The Watchtower* reports roughly a million members actively knocking on doors and some two million attending Kingdom Halls, politicians have no need to court the Jehovah's Witness vote because there is none. The entire membership is disenfranchised on orders from Brooklyn headquarters.

Ostensibly the reason for this is that "the whole world is lying in the power of the wicked one." (1 John 5:19 NWT) Satan the Devil controls all secular governments, so there is no point even trying to influence the course of public affairs. After all, so the JW reasoning goes, elections offer no real choice: Republican, Democrat, and independent candidates are all followers of Satan. Why is that? Because none of them are Jehovah's Witnesses, of course. (A member who ran for public office would be expelled the same as one who voted in an election.)

What the Witnesses themselves apparently fail to recognize about this view of the electoral process is that it is an example of circular reasoning: "Jehovah's Witnesses do not participate in politics, because everyone in politics is corrupt, because they are not Jehovah's Witnesses, because Jehovah's Witnesses do not participate in politics." Like a dog chasing its own tail, the argument goes around and around.

Although members will mouth these arguments and Bible verses to justify their stand, the real motivation behind JW abstinence from the political process is that the Governing Body in Brooklyn has commanded it to be so. If word were to come down from headquarters tomorrow to the effect that followers should now take part, voter registration offices worldwide would be swamped by the millions of Jehovah's Witnesses standing in line to participate—each one dutifully reciting the new argument and new interpretation of Bible verses supplied to support the new policy. The entire membership has done such an *en masse* about-face in the past on numerous occasions when policy reversals were decreed from above.

It is unlikely, however, that the leadership would alter its position on this issue in the foreseeable future, since it helps them accomplish a goal dear to the heart of all cult leaders who use mind control techniques on their followers. JW alienation from the political process plays an important part in keeping members estranged from mainstream society—an essential element in controlling their thinking. Rev. Jim Jones physically isolated his People's Temple followers at Jonestown in the jungle of Guyana, and David Koresh kept his Branch Davidians confined to their compound in Waco, Texas, but leaders of larger cults must find other means to produce the isolation required for mind control to function effectively. With their numbers reaching into the millions Jehovah's Witnesses cannot be separated into a Jonestown or a Waco compound, but the necessary mental isolation can be accomplished by cutting them off from interfaith worship services, from family holiday gatherings, from social clubs, and from sharing in any common cause politically with persons outside the sect.

Abstinence from voting allows JWs to declare with smug confidence that "we give our loyal support to God's kingdom government alone, not to any human rulers." The fact escapes their notice, however, that they are actually supporting a human organization ruled from New York rather than from heaven—a hierarchy ruling the lives of 12 million people in much the same way that various theocratic nation-states in the past have been ruled by priests claiming to represent God.

Interestingly, Jehovah's Witnesses *do* in fact vote among themselves to resolve questions and to appoint individuals to office within their own organization. Former Governing Body member Raymond Franz details in his book *Crisis of Conscience* the process by which that ruling council debates proposed doctrinal changes and puts them to the vote; if carried by a two-thirds majority, a "new truth"

225

is published in *The Watchtower* magazine as a product of Bible study or a revelation from God. During my eight years serving on the body of elders of a local congregation there were countless occasions when we called for a show of hands to decide an issue that lacked unanimous agreement or to vote our own chairman into office. Similarly, in order to fulfill statutory requirements for the ownership of property by a religious group, our congregation would periodically hold a business meeting to vote Kingdom Hall trustees into office. The congregation also voted on certain money matters and on questions such as whether to hold Thursday night meetings at 7:00 P.M. or 7:30 P.M.

What, then, is the difference between JWs voting for Kingdom Hall trustees and townspeople voting for selectmen? What is the difference between JWs voting to change meeting times and townspeople voting on a referendum question? The main difference seems to be that participation in Kingdom Hall politics will not get you run out of town, but participation in Town Hall politics will get you kicked out of Kingdom Hall and shunned by family and friends.

See Politics.

Zionism

Although *The Watchtower* magazine was originally titled *Zion's Watch Tower* Jehovah's Witnesses today disavow Zionism and "take the Biblical stand of being neutral" on Middle-Eastern political and territorial issues. (*Jehovah's Witnesses—Proclaimers of God's Kingdom,* page 141) This represents another significant doctrinal reversal, one in which "new light" contradicts "old light." (*See* New Light.)

Watchtower founder Charles Taze Russell was so strongly in favor of Jewish claims to Palestine that Jews continue to honor him today. As recently as 1986 a book was published titled *Pastor Charles Taze Russell: An Early*

American Christian Zionist by David Horowitz (New York: Philosophical Library). Under Russell's successor Joseph Rutherford the Watchtower Society at first maintained the same strong Zionist position. In 1925 it published Rutherford's book *Comfort for the Jews,* a compilation and amplification of his broadcast lectures on "Jews Returning to Palestine." Although this book claims to be "the first unbiased presentation of the subject from the Scriptural viewpoint," the Publisher's Foreword goes on to declare which side of the issue the Society's president favored: "JUDGE RUTHERFORD, known throughout the world as a friend of the Hebrew people, is vigorously supporting the claim of the Jews to the Holy Land." (page 3) Seven years later, in his 1932 book *Vindication,* volume 2, Rutherford abandoned that position.

Interestingly, the same Publisher's Foreword quoted above says further concerning Rutherford, "He is opposed to proselyting the Jews, holding that such is not only wrong but contrary to the Scriptures." (page 3) The Watchtower Society has reversed itself on this matter, too. Jehovah's Witnesses now actively seek to convert Jews, using literature produced by the Society for that specific purpose.

Jehovah's Witnesses today encounter hostility from both sides of the conflict: Jews see them as just another Christian group seeking converts, while anti-Semites doubt that they have really abandoned their Zionist stand. After all, who would believe that there could be such a dramatic reversal in a religion's tenets?

Frustrated? Keep Trying!

Do you feel frustrated? Does it seem you are getting nowhere in your conversations with Jehovah's Witnesses? Why is this so often the case?

The most common situation involves the Christian who wants to teach true Christian doctrine to the JW and who therefore starts out trying to do that—explaining the Trinity doctrine, and so on—using the Bible. Sooner or later he notices that he is just spinning his wheels, getting nowhere. Why? Because he has left out some necessary steps. His efforts are comparable to trying to teach calculus without first teaching algebra and arithmetic. You can't learn calculus without knowing algebra, and you can't learn algebra without knowing arithmetic. The JW can't learn Christian doctrine until he first sees that Watchtower doctrine is wrong. And he can't learn that Watchtower doctrine is wrong until he first sees through the organization's claim to divine authority as God's spokesman.

If you don't *first* prove the organization unreliable (documenting its false prophecies and back-and-forth changes) and then *second* reason verse-by-verse through the arguments the JW previously learned to support Watchtower doctrine, you can't expect much success with the *third* step of teaching Christian doctrine from Scripture.

Still, even when a Christian follows the proper steps and presents the material effectively, a JW may simply appear to shrug off the evidence. Why?

For a number of reasons Jehovah's Witnesses feel obligated to conceal any doubts or uncertainties they may have about their religion. First, of course, like all of us, they are handicapped by pride; we all hate to admit that we have been wrong. With JWs, however, there is much more at stake than wounded pride. They feel a strong obligation to bring you into "God's organization" and do not want to undermine their efforts by admitting uncertainty on their part. Even if you have succeeded in introducing a few doubts into the JW's mind, but he has not yet rejected the Watchtower organization, he doesn't dare admit those doubts. It would spoil *his* efforts to convert *you*.

Suppose, however, that what you said has actually gotten the Jehovah's Witness to question seriously whether he is in the true church. Will he admit to you that he has reached this stage? No! He cannot. He will still be afraid to express those thoughts before he has completely resolved the issue in his own mind. He knows that if he confesses his doubts to you, there is a possibility that this information about him may become public, and then he could be put on the spot by congregation elders—forced to declare himself either for or against the organization, before he has had the opportunity to fully explore the facts and reach a solid conclusion.

Therefore, don't give up. Even if the Witness has an answer for everything you say, and your arguments appear to be having no effect, you may actually be making much more headway than you think. As long as a JW is willing to listen, there is reason to hope that what you are saying is having a good effect.

In fact, even when you have *completely convinced* the JW that the Watchtower Society is a false prophet, and he is absolutely certain that he now wants to stop following it and to become a follower of Jesus, he may still hesitate to admit this to you. Why? Because he or she may be faced with the problem of helping a marriage mate or close friends or relatives to reach the same conclusions. Any premature announcement could result in the elders disfellowshiping the Witness, cutting off communication with these loved ones and blocking efforts to help them.

Once he has become convinced that you are right and that his religion is wrong, a JW may be willing to confide in you, but only if absolutely convinced of your reliability in keeping the matter private—your willingness for him to become a secret disciple like Nicodemus or Joseph of Arimathea. This need for secrecy may continue for months or even years, while the Witness works at freeing loved ones he could not bear to leave behind.

In other situations a lack of progress in discussions with a Jehovah's Witness may not be due to inadequacies in your presentation or the JW's fear of admitting error. Sometimes the JW simply does not want to hear the truth, or, hearing it, does not want to receive it. People have free will and the ability to make choices. Of the thousands in Galilee, Judea, and Samaria who heard Jesus preach in person, how many became his disciples? How many ignored the message, or even became angry and hated him? So, can we expect to have better results than Jesus did? The fault may not lie with our message, but rather with hearers who have closed their ears and their hearts.

Christ knew who would respond to his message and who would not, because he could read their hearts. Since we cannot do that, we should keep trying. If you have been skipping essential steps in reasoning with JWs, go back to the beginning and start over. My book *How to Rescue Your Loved One from the Watchtower* will help you to polish up your strategy and techniques and will give you material to use in undermining the sect's authority (step #1), and my other book *Jehovah's Witnesses Answered Verse by Verse* will help you untangle twisted reasonings (step #2). As long as the JW is willing to listen, it is a matter of patience and perseverance on your part.

Don't be discouraged by an apparent lack of progress. Breaking through to a Jehovah's Witness is like tunneling through a mountain. There is no visible indication that the tunnel has *almost* broken through—just the same pitch black darkness until suddenly you break through into the light of day.

The Lord knows who will eventually respond and who will not. We continue His work of sowing seed on all sorts of soil, cultivating it to the best of our ability. And, especially as regards witnessing to Jehovah's Witnesses, the words of Ecclesiastes 11:6 apply:

> "In the morning sow thy seed, and in the evening withhold not thine hand: for thou knowest not whether shall prosper, either this or that, or whether they both shall be alike good."

The JW who begins questioning and thirsting for truth may be forced to keep quiet about it for a while, and may not be able to encourage you with signs of progress, but when the time is ripe you will hear him praise the Lord!

Notes

[1] *Jehovah's Witnesses in the Divine Purpose* (Brooklyn: Watchtower Bible and Tract Society of New York, Inc., 1959) page 8.

[2] *Ibid.* Watchtower publications feature the name Jehovah's Witnesses with the "W" capitalized at times, but in lower case at other times. Another variation, Jehovah's Christian Witnesses, has also been used, but less frequently.

[3] *Apocalypse Delayed* by M. James Penton (Univ. of Toronto Press, 1985), page 17. Also, the October 5, 1985, *History Newsletter* of the Church of God General Conference (Oregon, Illinois), and the article "Benjamin F. Wilson and the 'Emphatic Diaglott'" by Paul M. Hatch, in the Church of God's magazine *The Restitution Herald*, June 15, 1964, later reprinted in the Christadelphian publication *Ecclesia*.

[4] These included, if I remember correctly, pages 494 and 499 of the August 15, 1968, *Watchtower* magazine, where a study article titled in all capital letters, "WHY ARE YOU LOOKING FORWARD TO 1975?" asked, "Are we to assume from this study that the battle of Armageddon will be all over by the autumn of 1975, and the long-looked-for thousand-year reign of Christ will begin by then?" The article assured readers that the date might be off by "only a difference of weeks or months, not years."

[5] The *Aid* book said, "At the age of 130 another son was born to her," making Eve's age the same as that given at Genesis 5:3 for Adam when Seth was born. The revised article in *Insight on the Scriptures* (page 772) changes this to "When Adam was 130 years old, Eve gave birth . . ."

Notes

[6]*Zion's Watch Tower,* August 1, 1910, page 4658, Society's reprints. Also, Vol. II of *The Great Pyramid Passages* by John Edgar and Morton Edgar, privately published in Glasgow, Scotland, in 1913, mentions on the unnumbered page facing page 1 that "copies may be procured by applying to . . . The Watch Tower Bible and Tract Society, 13 Hicks Street, Brooklyn, N.Y., United States of America."

Resources

Listed here are books, ministries, and support groups that will prove helpful in responding to Jehovah's Witnesses.

BOOKS

Apocalypse Delayed: The Story of Jehovah's Witnesses by M. James Penton (Toronto: University of Toronto Press, 1985)

Behind the Watchtower Curtain by David A. Reed (Southbridge, MA: Crowne Publications, 1989)

Blood on the Altar by David A. Reed (Amherst, NY: Prometheus Books, 1996)

Combatting Cult Mind Control by Steven Hassan (Rochester, VT: Park Street Press, 1988)

Crisis of Conscience by Raymond V. Franz (Atlanta: Commentary Press, 1983)

How to Rescue Your Loved One from the Watchtower by David A. Reed (Grand Rapids, MI: Baker Book House, 1989)

Index of Watchtower Errors by David A. Reed, Steve Huntoon, and John Cornell (Grand Rapids, MI: Baker Book House, 1990)

Jehovah's Witness Literature: A Critical Guide to Watchtower Publications by David A. Reed (Grand Rapids, MI: Baker Book House, 1993)

Jehovah's Witnesses Answered Verse by Verse by David A. Reed (Grand Rapids, MI: Baker Book House, 1986)

"No blood!" by David A. Reed (Assonet, MA: Comments from the Friends, 1995)

The Jehovah's Witnesses' New Testament by Robert H. Countess (Phillipsburg: Presbyterian and Reformed Publishing Company, 1982, 1987 edition)

Worse Than Waco by David A. Reed (Stoughton, MA: Comments from the Friends, 1993)

Why You Should Believe in the Trinity by Robert M. Bowman, Jr. (Grand Rapids: Baker Book House, 1990)

MINISTRIES AND SUPPORT GROUPS

Berean Christian Ministries, P.O. Box 1091, Webster, NY 14580. Literature, traveling speaker, 24-hour recorded message for JWs (716–872–3510).

Comments from the Friends, P.O. Box 819, Assonet, MA 02702. Quarterly publication, books, tapes, videos, traveling speaker, referrals to local contacts worldwide, 24-hour recorded message for JWs (508–584–4467). [This is the ministry of David A. Reed, author of this book.]

Free Minds, Inc., P.O. Box 3818, Manhattan Beach, CA 90266. Newsletter, books, tapes, traveling speaker, support group.

Freedom in Christ, P.O. Box 55, Mt. Gravatt, Queensland 4122, Australia. Newsletter, books, tapes, traveling speakers, support group.

Help Jesus Ministry, P.O. Box 3151, Aba, Abia State, Nigeria. Books, tracts, traveling speaker.

Hope Ministries, P.O. Box 841256, Pembroke Pines, FL 33084. Support group.

Intermountain Christian Ministries, P.O. Box 21322, Salt Lake City, UT 84121. Literature, counseling, traveling speaker, 24-hour message for JWs (801–942–0088).

JW Helpline, P.O. Box 83091, Milwaukee, WI 53223. Hotline for counseling and local referrals (1–800-WHY–1914).

Lovers of Truth, 129 Ballards Road, Dagenham, Essex RM10 9AR, England. Literature, traveling speakers, counseling.

MacGregor Ministries, P.O. Box 73, Balfour, B.C. V0G 1C0, Canada. Newsletter, books, tapes, tracts, traveling speakers.

Midwest Christian Outreach, P.O. Box 26, Rock Falls, IL 61071. Newsletter, traveling speakers, 24-hour recorded message for JWs (815–625–3678).

Personal Freedom Outreach, P.O. Box 26062, St. Louis, MO 63136. Newsletter, books, tapes, videos, traveling speakers.

Personal Freedom Outreach—East, R.D. 3, Box 127, Kunkletown, PA 18058. Books, tapes, annual ex-Witness convention.

Pioneer Ministries, P.O. Box 554, Timberville, VA 22853. Support group.

The Tyndales, Box 71, The Strand, Somerset West 7130, Cape Province, South Africa. Books, tracts, traveling speakers.

Watchman Fellowship, P.O. Box 74091, Birmingham, AL 35253. Newsletter, books, tracts, tapes, videos, traveling speakers.

Witness, Inc., P.O. Box 597, Clayton, CA 94517. Books, videos, tapes, tracts, traveling speakers. Child custody specialist.

World Cult Evangelism, P.O. Box 1961, Lawrenceville, GA 30246. Books, tracts, traveling speakers, 24-hour message for JWs (770-932-3806).

NOTE: Readers interested in obtaining originals or repro-ductions of out-of-print Watchtower materials and other books listed here that are not available through bookstores may direct their inquiries to the author:

David A. Reed
Comments from the Friends
P.O. Box 819
Assonet, MA 02702

Scripture Index

Genesis
1:2 115, 139, 170
5:3 18, 233
9:4 49
18:23–33 136
40:20–22 46

Exodus
6:3 143

Leviticus
3:17 49
7:23 49
7:26–27 49

Numbers
1:52
2:1 114
2:2 114

Deuteronomy
12:27 49
18:10–12 172
18:11 95
18:20–22 109, 110
18:22 110

1 Samuel
13:8–14 110
13:14 161

28:3 95
28:15 95
28:19 95

1 Kings
3:16–28 69

Nehemiah
2:1 78

Job
1:4 47
1:4–5 47–48
3:1–3 47

Psalms
45:16 42
83.18 143
86:14 215
146:3–4 93
146:4 93–94

Proverbs
4:14 167
4:18 167
4:19 167
18:13 33

Ecclesiastes
9:5 93, 94

9:10 93, 94
11:6 232
12:5 94
12:7 94
12:14 94

Isaiah
9:6 147, 173
10:20 148
10:21 148
12:2 143
14:9–10 95
26:4 143
43:10 144
43:10–11 116
44:6 116
44:8 116
48:12–13 116
63:10 139

Jeremiah
32:18 148

Ezekiel
4:6 36

Daniel
4:16–32 36
10:13 157, 158

Scripture Index

Scripture Index

Subject Index

Subject Index

Subject Index

Adventists and Millerites, 21–22, 25, 73, 81, 119, 167, 183; association with N. H. Barbour, 26; association with William Miller, 26; his belief in the deity of the Holy Spirit, 141; birth, 21; and the date of October 1914, 36–37, 38; death, 144; his espousal of Zionism 226–27; estranged from his wife, 154–55; as founder of JWs, 121, 124; and publication of JW literature, 201–5; and pyramidology, 186, 189, 191, 192, 193; venerated, 91

Russellism. *See* Russell, Charles Taze

Rutherford, Joseph F., 205–8; death, 38, 42; events in his life supposedly foretold in the Bible, 80; his espousal of pyramidology, 186; his espousal of Zionism, 227; as occupant of Beth-Sarim, 42; as originator of the "Great Crowd" teaching, 127, 130, 148-49; relationship with the JW Board of Directors, 124; his selection of the name "Jehovah's Witnesses," 144; his teaching about Pleiades, 180

Salvation, 208–9

Satan, 15, 16, 224

Second Coming, of Jesus Christ, 39, 122; as predicted by Charles Taze Russell, 24; as predicted by George Storrs, 20; as predicted by N. H. Barbour, 20, 22–23; as predicted by William Miller, 20. *See also* Parousia

Secrecy, of JWs, 89–90

Sexual intimacies, 156

Shunning, 59, 211–15

Smth (Professor), 193

Social problems, among JWs, 28–29

Soul & spirit, 215–17

Soul, nature of, 16

Stetson, George, 22

Storrs, George, 20

Subjection, of wife to husband, 16

Taylor, John, 193

Three Worlds, or Plan of Redemption, coauthored by Russell and Barbour, 140, 141

"Times of the Gentiles." *See* "Appointed times of the nations"

"Torture stake." *See* Cross, of Christ

Trinity, 97, 115, 217–19

Unity, 220–23

Voting, 181, 223–26. *See also* Politics

War. *See* Military service

Watch Tower, first issue, 201

Wilson, Benjamin, 23

You Can Live Forever in Paradise, as text for new JW converts, 175

Zionism, 226–27

Zion's Watchtower, first issue, 20, 201–2

Zion's Watchtower and Herald of Christ's Presence, first issue, 24, 118, 183

About the Author

David A. Reed became a baptized Jehovah's Witness in 1969. He served the Watchtower Society as a full-time minister, an elder, and a presiding overseer. Eventually, personal Bible reading caused him to question the organization's teachings, and this led to his formal expulsion in 1982.

After embracing biblical Christianity he began writing articles and tracts with the aim of evangelizing Jehovah's Witnesses. Today he publishes *Comments from the Friends*, a quarterly on the JWs. His books include:

How to Rescue Your Loved One from the Watchtower
Index of Watchtower Errors
Jehovah's Witness Literature—A Critical Guide to Watchtower Publications
Jehovah's Witnesses Answered Verse by Verse
Mormons Answered Verse by Verse (with ex-Mormon John R. Farkas)